Other books by Leon and Stanley Lobel

**MEAT**
**ALL ABOUT MEAT**

# THE LOBEL BROTHERS' MEAT COOKBOOK

## Leon and Stanley Lobel

### with Jon Messmann

CORNERSTONE LIBRARY
New York

Published by Cornerstone Library, Inc.,
a Simon & Schuster Division of
Gulf & Western Corporation
Simon & Schuster Building
Rockefeller Center
1230 Avenue of the Americas
New York, NY 10020

CORNERSTONE LIBRARY and colophon
are trademarks of Simon and Schuster,
registered in the U.S. Patent and
Trademark Office.

Library of Congress Cataloging in Publication Data


Lobel, Leon.
   The Lobel brothers' meat cookbook.

   1. Cookery (Meat)   2. Cookery, International.
I. Lobel, Stanley, joint author.   II. Title.
TX749.L64        641.6′6        79-26060

ISBN 0-346-12472-7

To my very interesting and wonderful partner in marriage,
  Anita
To our 5th generation and future partner in our business, my
  son Evan
To my two very talented girls, Linda and Wendy;
To my son-in-law Dennis (our agent and lawyer)
To my brother Stanley who shared his sweat, and helped create
  what we have today,
And to all my friends, and to all those everywhere, who share
  our love for the best.

LEON LOBEL

It is with true love and devotion that I dedicate my book to the
most wonderful woman in the world, my wife Evelyn, and to
the dearest sons a man could want, David and Mark, who have
made me so very proud.

STANLEY LOBEL

# CONTENTS

# FOREWORD

Whether Leon and Stanley Lobel are cutting meat or selling it, writing about it or talking about it, rendering advice on it, or cooking it, these things become clear: They know what they are doing and they love it.

And it's probably those qualities which make the brothers so refreshing in these days of indifferent service and dying craftsmanship.

The Lobel brothers display their elegance and professional style when dealing with their customers. Leon Lobel is a slim and gentle man but there's authority in his soft speech. Stanley Lobel is medium-tall and has a straightforward manner that puts people immediately at ease.

The Lobels are the fourth generation in the family to be in the meat business and their shop at 82nd Street and Madison Avenue, on New York City's swank upper East Side, is a showplace of talent and artistry.

The brothers and their hired staff, whose training has been impeccable, proceed to trim the beef, bone the lamb, truss the poultry, or pound the veal while the rich and not-so-rich gape through the windows.

In their spare time on weekends, Leon and Stanley Lobel write a newspaper column about meat and in a short period of time have gained a devoted following of readers of Gannett Westchester-Rockland-Fairfield newspapers.

The Lobels know their customers and greet them by name. Very little money appears to change hands over the counter, as the Lobels offer the service of a charge account. They don't have too much trouble with nonpaying customers, probably because of their straightforward habit of closing out accounts which are overdue and gentle refusal to open accounts for those whom they consider poor risks.

9

Who shops in the store? Customers include recognized celebrities and those whose power is wielded quietly, those who easily can afford the best and those who will sacrifice for it.

In comes a couple, in search of chickens to simmer in preparation for a casserole. The man requests a stewing chicken.

"A stewing chicken is a farce," says Stanley bluntly, "let me give you one of my pullets."

And the customers in that store don't ask "Tell me, Stanley, why is a stewing chicken a farce?" After all, who questions God?

To talk about the Lobels and not mention their prices is unfair.

The Lobels charge plenty. While one of the fanciest shops in town may be selling paper-thin veal scaloppine for a whopping cost the Lobels are asking 25 percent more. Their chickens cost three times as much as ones from the supermarket. Those are just two examples, but since they range from the least expensive to the most, they probably are good ones.

The customers don't bat an eyelash at paying the prices. Why? For one thing, they're getting quality—probably the finest New York City has to offer. The second reason is, they are getting service—the classic, old-fashioned service, which decrees the customer is king—and that service includes the way the meat is cut and wrapped, the cooking instructions the Lobels love to give, the charge accounts, and the careful, time-consuming attention to the indecisive customer.

And the customers are getting something else: the unabashed joy the Lobels have in seeing them come into the store and the sense of history that hovers over the chopping boards. There's Father Morris Lobel peering down from the walls and young Evan Lobel is the fifth generation to join the business.

It's a classy shop all right; it's the quintessential New York store we all look for and seldom find.

And that class is reflected in this book. The Lobels write about meat with as much care as they wait on a customer.

They have done extensive research to provide us with background of their recipes. They take us out of our homes to different parts of the world. They have tested and retested each recipe. And because the instructions, tips, and hints come from the Lobels, with their five generations of family pride, you just know those recipes are going to be the best. And they are.

VARIAN H. CASSAT
Food Editor
Gannett Westchester-Rockland Newspapers

# INTRODUCTION

When the first man or woman charred the first leg of mastodon, the new taste sensation was undoubtedly first greeted with grunts of awe, then pleasure. Others came to see, to taste, to partake; and lo, from a furtive, solitary eater tearing off bites of raw meat in a corner somewhere man was changed into a social creature. The *meal* came into existence, a time when several people gathered together around the fire to share the cooked meat. And from that early moment, man departed from all other creatures in still another way.

Much has been written about the differences (or lack of differences) between human beings and animals. Yet largely ignored has been that one, salient difference involving food: Only man feels the need to be grateful. No other creature offers gratitude for its food. Only man offers thanks and uses his precious life-sustaining food as a symbol of that gratitude. No one knows why this is so. Primitive altars, built in fields and forests, have supplied evidence that meat has been central to man's needs, physically and spiritually. It has been the most precious thing he had to offer in worship, matched only in some primitive societies by the offering of life itself.

Man became a cook before he became anything else—before he became a builder, an artist, a decorator of caves, a tiller of the soil, a potter, or a maker of tools and certainly before he became a chemist. Cooking and chemistry have always had a relationship, as cooking is chemistry. As early man began to cook his meat, he built his fires bigger and hotter. A moment came when the intense heat began to melt the malachite under it. The copper inside the malachite began to soften, then to ooze out to snake along the ground. Later, while still warm, the copper could be handled and shaped, and when it cooled it kept its shape. Man the cook had become man the chemist. He had learned to extract metal from the earth's ore—one of the earliest examples of applied chemistry. From this discovery came cooking utensils to make meat even more savory.

Other foods were added to the basic meat, such as the kernels of wild grasses and wheat, which man learned to extract through the use of a hot, flat stone. Just as the knowledge of applied chemistry grew, so the knowledge of the chemistry of cooking increased. Man discovered how to boil meat by using hot stones placed in pits of water to create boiling water. American settlers found the Indians still using this very same method with their buffalo and deer meat. It is not surprising, then, that up through medieval times recipes were often called formulas and that as late as 1822, Dr. William Kitchiner in his volume, *The Cook's Oracle*, wrote, "A cook must be as particular to proportion her fire . . . as a chemist."

Since the time that the first cook roasted the first piece of meat, those members of the tribe, clan, group, and community who devoted themselves to making food more pleasurable and tastier have been held in special regard as the keepers of charismatic gifts—gifts given to one to share with many. In ancient Sumer, only the priests were permitted to make butter at the sacred dairy farms. Holy men soon became the only ones allowed to offer the sacrifice of meat to the gods. Egyptian priests, according to the Greek chronicler, Herodotus, subsisted on a special diet of a daily supply of goose, beef, and bread made from sacred grain, plus wine.

In ancient times the connection between meat, life, and worship existed in all societies everywhere. Dining rooms formed a regular part of Syrian temples. In Mesopotamia, shrines were built that included granaries. In Egypt, a bull was ritually slain after prayers to the gods (with accompanying libations); it was then stuffed with raisins, honey, bread, figs, myrrh, and frankincense and finally burned. The priests offering the sacrifice then dined on the remains of the carcass. So from the very beginning, meat has been more than simply a food. Man's use of meat has been both a result and a reflection of his existence, and his history—from philosophies to fashions, morals to manners—may be traced by observing the different ways man has regarded, prepared, and cooked meat.

Once the human race began to lift itself out of the earliest mists of primitive existence, it began to drift into separate groups, individual tribes, clans, and communities. Man the hunter and wanderer became less nomadic, and he began to establish roots in communities. Distinct cultures were evolved, followed by the first seeds of regional cooking. All the while, meat continued to be man's basic food.

The area of the Tigris and the Euphrates Valley has been called the cradle of civilization. Out of this vast area came the civilizations of the Nile, ancient Egypt, the Mesopotamians, the Babylonians, the peoples of Asia Minor, and the Hebrew culture of Israel. From this cradle flowed learning that eventually reached, via the Greeks and the conquering Romans, what today we call Europe. The grandest of the Nile River civilizations was that of the ancient Egyptians. Some of their contributions that have filtered down to this very century include a knowledge of herbs, some 250 varieties classified as to their dietary and medicinal values, and a knowledge of farming methods, which have been passed on to hundreds of generations.

Perhaps because so many Egyptian friezes depict the sowing and reaping of wheat and maize, ancient Egypt has often been called an agrarian society. Certainly the rich topsoil of the Nile deltas did lend itself to farming. But meat was a staple of Egyptian diet. Egyptians raised a very hardy strain of longhorn cattle and in time imported other strains of beef. They presaged modern feeding methods by grain-feeding their beef. And long before the Strasbourg goose they were force-feeding their fowl. They also enjoyed the pâté de foie gras ages before the French Court.

The high grasses and marshes of the Nile valley attracted birds of all kinds, and a bird-hunting party is commonly depicted on Egyptian friezes. Poultry of all kinds became an important part of the Egyptian diet, including geese, ducks, quail, doves, thrushes, pigeons, and guinea hens. Inscriptions mention forty-eight different varieties of baked meats, hardly the sign of an agrarian civilization.

The Egyptians were the first to extensively use figs, apricots, kumquats, grapes, and other fruits in combination with meat dishes to heighten taste and add succulence. Meat was part of the Egyptian enjoyment of the good life, a basic food turned into a food of pleasure and playful inventiveness only possible in a worldly and sensual society.

In sharp contrast to Egypt was the world of the ancient Greeks. Although they borrowed many of their customs from the civilization of the pharaohs, the resemblance ended there. Ancient Greece was a civilization of heroes. The Greek gods and goddesses were heroic figures shot through with human faults. The great dialogues and debates in the Greek forums were intellectual contests filled with a kind of mental heroics. Their Olympic games were physical tests of man against man and man against himself, subjecting the body to heroic stresses and strains. There are no unheroic statues in Greek sculpture, and even their tragedies, as defined by Aristotle, had to be of heroic proportions to be worthy of the name *tragedy*.

It was little wonder, then, that the Greek dinner often became an all-night contest of eating, drinking, and debating. The one who did best in all three areas received the accolades of his fellows, when they were revived enough to give them. As the Athenian poet and social critic Eubulus noted, ''I pray you, where in Homer is the Chief who e'er eat fish, or anything but beef?'' And Athenaeus of Naucratis, who is famous for his piece of intellectual gamesmanship—*The Banquet of the Learned (Deipnosophistae)*, a fictional banquet of food and cerebral fireworks—said that Homer told his heroes to eat only ''viands of simple kinds'' and to never put anything before his princes ''but meat as was calculated to make them vigorous in body and mind.''

But meat was the food of the heroic not just because of its nutritional benefits. The Greek peninsula was, and is, a rugged and severe land—mountainous, dry, and inhospitable to the raising of beef cattle. Beef was therefore reserved as a reward for the heroic; in short, meat was a gastronomic reflection of the philosophy of the entire Hellenic order.

The Romans, who seemed to want to outdo the Greeks in everything, did not carry on as close a dialogue of worship as had the Greeks. The Romans shifted the main thrust of their adulations from gods and goddesses to earthly beings —their mighty military commanders, their great soldiers, their emperors. Conquerors, colonizers, and road-builders —the Romans went far from their homeland on their adventures and brought back not only slaves but also cattle, spices, fruits, cheeses, and wines. They also brought back many new and exotic manners of cooking meat with the new spices they uncovered. Rome became a composite of many cultures, and certain, well-educated slaves were held in high esteem for their specialized knowledge. A Roman feast was a place of gastronomic delight. One feast was described as being made up of "all the products of land and sea, river and air" (*Julius Caesar*, I, 2).

The ostrich, mightiest and most powerful of birds, was considered fit for an emperor, and ostrich fat was used as a drug. Beef and pork also were food for the mighty. Imperial Rome, the center of much of the world and the marketplace of the Mediterranean, dined on beef, lamb, boar, suckling pig, fallow deer, gazelle, roebuck, and every kind of winged creature. Imperial Rome believed in imperial meat, and its tables signified its status as a conquering nation.

But in time, the glory of Rome was no more. With the fall of the Empire, all the refinements of the table vanished. Roman rule and order gave way, and the culture that was Rome was swept away with it—the cultivated lands, the vineyards, and the tenant-farmed fields. Forest and marsh rose again, and only the great Roman roads remained, as some of them have to this very day. By the beginning of medieval times, much of Europe was reforested, becoming once again a home for deer, wild boar, and bear. The roasting spit soon became the primary method of cooking. The Dark Ages were upon the land, and a kind of primitive spartanism held forth in the kitchens as well as in the minds of men. An empire of vastness gave way to feudal fiefdoms, each a separate enclave of power.

The Christian ascetic had grown more powerful, and his spirit inveighed against the sensualist dining that had been practiced by the Romans and Greeks. Still, even an ill wind does some good. Our modern appreciation of the true flavor of good meat can be said to have had its roots in the return to simpler forms of cooking and roasting. The Dark Ages did, albeit unintentionally, modify some of the overrefinements of Roman cooking.

Today, it is generally believed that knowledge, the written word itself and a great body of learning, was kept alive through the Dark Ages by churchmen: the monks and friars. They became, because of their spiritual and physical isolationism, the trustees of erudition as well as arcane secrets. And it was these same clerics who kept the traditions of refined cooking alive.

Monastic orders grew, and each monastery became an oasis of culture. Monks farmed, tilled, and seeded—behind their walls, first, then outside them. They developed the art of the vintner; they became the makers of fine brandy, bakers of bread, and gatherers of honey. New orchards and vineyards were planted and old ones were revived.

In an unstable era, monasteries were islands of stability. The Benedictines saw labor in the fields as an extension of Christian duty, and the monastic orders soon occupied a special role as spiritual guardians and material providers. From the tenth to the twelfth centuries, Europe experienced some forty famines and various onslaughts of plague and pestilence, and the monastery was often the only source of food for the surrounding countryside. Feudal lords, more interested in fighting and plundering, did little to maintain the food supply chain. Rather, it was the monasteries that managed to maintain some semblance of supply. The time-honored legend that the traveler could always find food and lodging at a monastery was rooted in practical fact as well as in the spirit of charity.

The Benedictine monastery on Lake Constance contained not only the usual herb gardens and orchards but also a vegetable garden and areas for baking, for preserving fruit, for brewing, for storing grain, and for raising beef and lamb. Almost every kind of herb, vegetable, and fruit that could be grown was produced there. The Cistercians had farms for breeding horses, cattle, sheep, and geese. The Franciscans and Dominicans had similar establishments.

From the monasteries the secrets of refined cooking appeared. When the spirit of the Renaissance began to invest every aspect of life, it had its fullest flowering in Italy—the home of many of the great monastic orders where the culinary flame was kept burning. As direct descendants of the Romans, the Italians brought the enjoyment of fine cooking back to Europe. It was fitting that perhaps the most influential of Renaissance cookbooks was *The Cooking Secrets of Pope Pius V*. Written by Bartolomeo Scappi and published in 1570, it contained such sophisticated recipes as legs of goat, stuffed goose in Lombard style, songbirds roasted on the spit with sliced tongues over them, soup of pigeon and almond paste, and similar examples of the cook's art.

It must also be remembered that after the Seljuk Turks had swept almost to the gates of Vienna before falling back, the Moorish-Saracen occupation lasted far longer in Spain and southern Italy than the mere presence of soldiers. The culinary imprints the Saracens brought—including knowledge of the delights of the ageless olive, lemon, and dates; the uses of olive oil, and a vast array of spices and seasonings—became part of the cooking of the region. The Moorish and Eastern ways with meat were assimilated, ingested, and stamped with a new mark, and it was this culinary sophistication that the Italians of the Renaissance brought north to the Continent and that the French embraced.

The delicacy and variety of cooking meat lay with the Italians of the Renaissance until France became the center of political sophistry, fashion, etiquette, and *haut monde* in almost every area of living. Just as the Romans had to be better than the Greeks, so the French felt constrained to outdo the

Italians. France became the land of embellishments (many said excesses) in all things, from dress to dining, from l'amour to license, from royal misbehavior to clerical machinations.

Again, we need only look at the treatment of meat to see that a new culture had developed. Even in their guilds, the French embellished the art of cooking. Chefs had formed societies in other lands and at other times, but in France there were not only the *cuisiniers* but the *charcutiers*, the sausage and pork and smoked meats specialists; the *rotisseurs*, the specialists in roasting meat, poultry, and venison; the *sauciers*, those chefs whose province it was to invent the sauces that accompanied almost all meat. Sauces are still the hallmark of French cooking. As the master chef Escoffier said centuries later, "A sauce must fit the roast as a tight-fitting skirt fits a woman."

The French influence is perhaps best exemplified by a dinner given by the Duc de Richelieu for a small group of Hanoverian royalty captured during the Seven Years' War. The host's field supplies were meager: one carcass of beef and vegetables and a few fruits. Yet the dinner menu consisted of beef consommé, hors d'oeuvre of bits of beef dressed in different ways, a beef rump with vegetables, side dishes of oxtail with chestnut purée, beef tongue, fillets of beef braised with celery, beef marrow on toast, *cervelle* (brains) with orange juice, and other similar delicacies.

Such inventiveness reflected a country where the land furnished almost every kind of food in ample supply. Sophisticated palates seldom emerge from cultures where the soil must be scraped for food—imaginative cooking, yes, and often remarkable and specialized dishes carried to perfection, but not sophisticated palates. In post-Renaissance France, more than perhaps in any other country, it was not only the ruling classes that had an appreciation of fine food but also the middle and lower classes, a distinction that has carried to this day.

As France emerged as a power, its influence was felt in politics, fashion, music, manners, and morals. The English have always had a strange love-hate relationship with the Continent and things Continental, especially things French. Perhaps the emotional residue of 1066 still lingered. The Norman knights who invaded England brought new manners to the Saxons. Before the Normans came, the Saxons roasted whole oxen and tore the meat from the carcass half-raw. The Norman knights, on the other hand, sliced pieces of meat from the animal and then cooked them in the fashion of our steaks. In any case, England embraced the French ways as a reluctant lover, eager yet uncertain. It did the same with its alliances with France.

When Tudor England turned from Europe after Henry VIII broke with Rome, many viewed this, in terms of English cuisine, as a step backward. Backward or not, an insular pride was immediately encouraged and once more was instantly reflected in the preparation and cooking of meat. The Englishman returned to his roasts with renewed vigor. Beef and mutton became a national rallying cry. The English yeoman attained new status under the Tudor reign and his eating habits a kind of growling, bulldog pride. As Thomas Fuller wrote in the *Worthies*, "At our yeoman's table you shall have . . . no meat disguised with strange sauces . . . but solid, substantial food." This culinary echo of political attitudes became endemic in English cuisine, though in fairness it should be said that the fourth century Greek epicure, Archestratus of Athens, also railed against the drowning of meat in sauces: "Many are the ways and many the recipes for dressing hares, but this is best of all, to place before a hungry set of guests a slice of roasted meat fresh from the spit, hot, seasoned only with plain, simple salt. . . . All other ways are quite superfluous, such as when cooks pour a lot of sticky, clammy sauce upon it."

Two hundred years after the Tudors drew England back unto itself, the English, who had by then established themselves as beefeaters, still raged against the way Italy, France, and Spain treated meat. Meat traced the political, cultural, and geographic convolutions of mankind's path through history. The agronomy of the land and the acuity of those who lived on the land was mirrored in the preparation of their basic food the world over.

The interest in Chinese food has grown tremendously in recent years, especially Chinese cooking methods like stir-frying. Whatever its dietary and gustatory merits, this method of cooking developed because of certain geographical and cultural conditions, not because of any Oriental culinary wisdom. The Chinese peasant was hampered by the vast reaches of China, its protracted droughts and vast plains. He was also confined by the lack of transportation facilities. In the plains of provincial China, firewood was at a premium, both in quantity and in the ability to fetch it. The timber in the mountainous areas was as unreachable to most peasant families as were the palaces of the Kublai Khan.

Fuel in China, then, had to be used with care and sparingly, and so a method of cooking meat was developed that allowed for brief cooking times. The Western way of slow-roasting meats was therefore out of the question, and sides of beef were simply not available. Other dishes that required a great deal of time and subtlety to cook were also eliminated by practical necessities. The Chinese turned to preparing meat in small pieces—cutting it in strips, dicing it, or shredding it. They did the same with their vegetables and thus created a cooking method that made for quickness, permitting them to use as little of their precious firewood as possible under their saucer-shaped woks. This style of cooking was compatible with the harsh and spare lives of the Chinese peasant.

So in the East, just as everywhere else, meat and human existence have interlocked, practically, culturally, and spiritually, from antiquity to the present times. Perhaps nowhere does this appear more tellingly than in the Bible. In Genesis, God tells Noah, "Every moving thing that liveth shall be meat for you." And, later, Isaac says to Esau, "Take, I pray thee, thy weapons, thy quiver and thy bow and go out into the field and take me some venison; and make me savory meat such as I love and bring it to me, that I may eat; that my soul may bless thee before I die." In Leviticus: "And thou shalt bring the meat offering . . . unto the Lord. . . . It is an offering made by fire of a sweet savor unto the Lord . . . a thing most holy of the offerings of the Lord made by fire."

In Proverbs, the mark of a good woman is that she "riseth in the night and giveth meat to her household and a portion to her maidens." In the first book of Kings, we are told of Elijah who "went in the strength of that meat, forty days and forty nights unto Horeb the mount of God."

In the New Testament meat is still basic to man's existence, "for the workman is worthy of his meat." It is but one more aspect of a more encompassing philosophy. In a letter to the Corinthians, Paul says, "Meat commandeth us not to God for neither if we eat are we the better, neither, if we eat not, are we the worse." And in Hebrews he wrote, "It is a good thing that the heart not be established with meat but with grace."

Meat and mankind continue on together, but something else has been added—a shift in philosophic emphasis. But whether the heart be established with grace or meat or both, we can see that modern man has raised his favorite food to the new heights and with good reason. At no time in history has the knowledge of animal husbandry, agricultural skills and the technologies of transportation and production reached the level they now enjoy. Now we can put on the table almost any kind of meat we desire. No longer need the buffalo be virtually wiped out by overhunting, or the antelope decimated. No longer need we destroy any species of animal or bird to supply our needs. This achievement is remarkable and is one that opens new doors of enjoyment for all people everywhere.

Different cultures have produced a vast collection of recipes with distinctive character. Like people, every cuisine, every dish, has its roots, its own story, its reason for existence. Knowledge adds new dimensions to pleasure. This truly epicurean inheritance is given us to be used, understood, and enjoyed. This book is a celebration of that heritage and of today's freedom and ability to enjoy it to the fullest.

To include all cuisines in this book was impossible and some, such as the Oriental, are so voluminous and varied as to take a work of their own. But in compiling this survey, and tracing the continuous relationship between meat and mankind, one fact reaffirmed itself again and again. The skillet and society have evolved together; the roast is a reflection of culture, geography, and politics.

In the June 1888 issue of *Century* magazine, the pioneer nutritionist, W. O. Atwater, speculating on the relationship of meat in particular to the human condition, wondered "whether there may not be, between the intellectual, social and moral force of its people, and the dietary usages of which those here are instanced, an important connection, one that reached down deep into the philosophy of human living."

Interestingly, it has been discovered that a key substance, choline, found primarily in meat, has a heretofore unimagined effect on the activity of the nerve impulses in the brain, especially in the formation of memory. Today, science has given new credence and authority to Atwater's words in praise of meat. To that, human history and the pleasures of the palate have added their own affirmation.

In seeing history through the kitchen, it soon became apparent that culinary roots developed, overlapped, flowed together, and separated with the same fluidity as human roots. Dishes repeat themselves in different places, sometimes with only the name changed. Therefore, in compiling the recipes here, every effort has been made to retain the authenticity of each while allowing for the facts of modern cooking and contemporary marketing. In short, we have eliminated those parts of the recipes that begin with "Look for a fat-tailed sheep" and have retained the rest.

We have also tried to avoid those dishes most generally and widely included in other cookbooks, or if they have been offered here, it has been done with a different touch, an added *saveur*. A comprehensive exploration of every style of meat cookery would fill volumes. So rather than include "token" dishes from everywhere we have confined ourselves to those major regions where culinary individuality most clearly reflected social, political, and cultural developments.

In classifying dishes, we have followed the root patterns of those dishes. For this reason, the great dishes of the Bible lands and Jewish heritage have been included in the chapter, "Jewish Cooking," for most all the truly indigenous dishes have a religious origin.

Charles Lamb, the essayist, wrote about the custom of saying grace before meals and attributed its origin to primitive times and "the hunter-state of man when dinners were precarious things and a full meal was something more than a common blessing." He said: "I own that I am disposed to say grace upon twenty other occasions in the course of the day besides my dinner. I want a form [of grace] for setting out upon a pleasant walk, for a moonlight ramble, for a friendly meeting or a solved problem. Why have we none for books, those spiritual repasts—a grace before Milton—a grace before Shakespeare—a devotional exercise to be said before reading *The Faerie Queen?*"

To those sentiments, we say amen. We talk about meat in terms of history and present recipes, and we do so in the spirit of Charles Lamb. We hope you will view *The Lobel Brothers' Meat Cookbook* as a kind of grace for the senses and the intellect.

# 1
# ASIA MINOR

MANKIND'S first cultures evolved from what has been called the cradle of civilization: the twin valleys of the Euphrates and the Nile. The countries we know today as Iran, Iraq, Syria, Lebanon, Israel, Egypt, Saudi Arabia, and Turkey were once known by other names: Persia, Turkestan, Mesopotamia, Babylonia, Palestine, Assyria, Chaldea, and Sumer. Not only have the names of the nations changed but the land has changed its character. Where today there is sand and barren soil there once was a land where goats, sheep, oxen, chicken, ducks, and geese were plentiful; where figs, cucumbers, olives, dates, grapes, and honey were staples. Misuse of the land and the tramp of conquering armies changed all that. The land was unable to support the modest herds of grazing cattle and the other game. But the land still lay between the trade routes of India, Africa, and Europe, heir to all the spices and herbs of the East and at one time to the meat and fowl of the West. That heritage remained in the traditional passage of culinary knowledge. When the land could no longer support the variety of animals, today's predominant mark of Middle Eastern cooking came into being —the use of lamb, mutton, and poultry.

Sheep, it was found, could thrive on land where no ox or cow could long survive and consequently became the staple meat in Asia Minor. Because much of the lamb and nearly all of the mutton was tough, stringy, and exceedingly strong in flavor, cooks used wine, spices, and herbs to create a tenderizing marinade. A cuisine that turned lamb and mutton into delicious and nutritious food thus came into existence.

Chicken also became a mainstay in Asia Minor. Diced or cubed lamb, mutton, and chicken also had entirely practical origins, as the cut-up meat marinated better and more quickly. It could also be handled more easily in the big earthen pots and iron kettles where meat was prepared. Eating was a communal affair. Most of the men came to eat from their tasks of herding in the mountains or in the villages where they labored at a trade. Dinnertime varied from day to day. In addition, the man of the house might bring guests at any unexpected time in accordance with Arabic hospitality. The cut-up diced meat could be stored in small-necked earthen jars for long periods to be brought out whenever the occasion demanded.

Their ways of preparing and cooking meat and indeed the nature of the meat itself mirrored a land that grew harsher as it grew older. But it also mirrored a people who took what they had and made it into what they lacked, who turned the gastronomic limitations forced on them by geography and nature into the pleasures of a communal meal created with inventiveness and love.

Out of the Middle East came the first of mankind's many movable feasts. Out of that heritage came the first examples of how man's use of meat evolved out of the character and climate of his environment. Today, we can enjoy the dishes that have been handed down to us from the first culinary cradle in many ways almost unchanged.

# Celery Stew
(*Khoresh Karafs*)

*Khoresh* is a stew of meat or fowl in which vegetables, fruits, or almost any other ingredient is mixed. *Karafs* is the Arabic word for *celery*. Woven garlands of wild celery have been found in Egyptian tombs.

> 1½ pounds beef chuck, bottom round, or rump roast, cut into 1-inch cubes
> 8 tablespoons butter
> 2 medium-sized onions, chopped
> ½ teaspoon pepper
> 1 teaspoon cinnamon
> ½ teaspoon nutmeg
> 2½ cups water
> 1½ cups parsley, chopped
> 5 cups celery, diced
> 1 teaspoon lemon juice

Melt 4 tablespoons of the butter in a 3-quart kettle. Add the onion, pepper, cinnamon, and nutmeg. Stir and put in the meat. Turn the meat often until browned on all sides. Add the water and cook, covered, over a medium heat for 1 hour, or until the meat is tender.

Ten minutes before the meat is done, melt the remainder of the butter in a skillet and add the parsley and celery. Sauté for 7 minutes, then combine the contents of the skillet with the meat in the kettle. Add the lemon juice, stir, and simmer (covered) for 10 minutes.

SERVES 4.

*Serve with rice or plain noodles.*

# Khorsh Geimah

The people of ancient Persia had no freezers but they did have the *geimah*, a way of preserving meat for unexpected guests. Meat was cut into ½- to 1-inch pieces, sautéed in butter and seasonings, and stored in narrow-necked earthen jugs kept in a cool place. When unexpected visitors arrived, the Persian mistress of the house dipped into her earthen jugs for the amount of *geimah* she needed, then recooked it mixed with vegetables, fruits, or whatever. It is a custom still in use.

> 1½ pounds beef chuck, boneless pot roast, heel of
>     round, or shank, cut into ½-inch pieces
> 6 tablespoons shortening
> 1 large onion, minced
> 1½ teaspoons salt
> 1 teaspoon pepper
> ½ teaspoon cinnamon
> ½ teaspoon turmeric
> ½ teaspoon nutmeg
> 3 cups water
>    Juice of 2 limes
> ½ cup yellow split peas
> 2 medium-sized potatoes, peeled and diced

In a 3-quart pot, melt 3 tablespoons of the shortening. Add the onion and meat. Mix the seasonings together, add them to the pot, and stir thoroughly. Sauté the meat slowly until it is browned on all sides. Pour the water and lime juice into pot, stir thoroughly, and simmer for 25 minutes. Add the split peas and simmer for another 25 minutes.

Fry the peeled and diced potatoes in the remainder of the shortening. Ten minutes before the *geimah* is done, add the fried potatoes and stir.

SERVES 4.

*Rice and watercress salad make good accompaniments.*

# Kofte on Skewers—Turkish Version
*(Kufteh Kabob in Persia)*

Ground meat on a skewer is a popular and economical dish throughout the Middle East. The basic dish is subject to minor variations according to the country or ethnic group.

1 pound beef or lamb, well ground
1 large onion, minced
1 large egg
½ teaspoon thyme
1 teaspoon garlic salt
½ teaspoon white pepper
½ tablespoon olive oil

Put the meat, onion, egg, thyme, garlic salt, and pepper into a bowl. Mix thoroughly. Rub olive oil on the palms of both hands and then divide the mixture into 4 parts, each the size of a fat bread stick. Carefully push 1 skewer through each piece of shaped meat. Grill or place 3 inches from the broiler flame and turn frequently. Cook about 6 to 10 minutes.

SERVES 4.

*Serve with tomatoes, cold or broiled, and crusty bread.*

# Pomegranate Soup

This dish is a far cry from what we of the West normally call soup. In old Asia Minor, *soup* and *meal* were more often than not one and the same thing. Soup was a robust, filling dish.

The Persian term for cook is *Ash-paz*, which translates as "the maker of the soup." *Ash-paz-khaneh* is Persian for kitchen, or "the home of the cook." Pomegranate soup is light pink in color with a delicate taste. It is said that it may be kept for three to four days, the flavor improving with each day.

> ¾ pound beef chuck or round, ground
> 1 small onion, grated
> 1 teaspoon cinnamon
> 1 teaspoon pepper
> 8 cups water
> ¾ cup rice
> ½ teaspoon salt
> 1 cup spinach, chopped
> 1 cup parsley, chopped
> 1 cup scallions, chopped
> 4 to 6 pomegranates, enough to furnish 2 cups of seeds
> or 1½ cups of juice
> ¼ cup sugar
> 1½ teaspoons mint, dried or flakes
> 1 teaspoon lime juice (optional)

In a mixing bowl, put the beef, onion, ½ teaspoon of the cinnamon, and ½ teaspoon of the pepper. Mix well and form into small meatballs (walnut-sized).

Put the water into a 3-quart kettle. Add the rice and salt and cook over a medium heat for 15 minutes. Add the spinach, parsley, and scallions and stir well. Cook for an additional 15 minutes. Add the meatballs, pomegranate juice or seeds, and sugar. Cook for 15 to 20 minutes.

While the mixture is cooking, make a powder of the dried mint in a small bowl (use a pestle or rub it between the palms of both hands). Add the remainder of the cinnamon and pepper and mix well. When the soup is done, add the mint seasoning and stir. Taste. If the soup is too sweet, add the lime juice a little at a time. Serve hot.

Serves 4 to 5.

# Kibby

*Kibby* is the national dish of Syria and Lebanon. It is made with meat and hand-ground, cracked wheat, called *bulgur* (or *burghol*) in Arabic. The farmers (*fallaheen*) bring the baskets of grain to the river for washing. The *bulgur* is then boiled in kettles and set out in the sun to dry. When dry, it is ground in a mill, and the kernels are sorted and then hand-ground again. Sunday dinner in a Syrian household must include *Kibby Neeyee*. *Bulgur* is sold in the United States in three ways: fine, medium, and coarse.

> 2 pounds beef chuck or round, ground
> 2 cups cracked wheat (*bulgur*), fine
> 1½ cups cold water
> 1 large onion, minced
> ½ teaspoon pepper
> 1 teaspoon salt
> Melted butter

This recipe calls for the meat to be uncooked, as in *tartare*.

Using a mixing bowl, rinse the wheat in the cold water. Then drain the water from the wheat, squeezing it by hand. Add the meat, onion, pepper, and salt. Using a meat grinder or a food processor, grind all the ingredients twice. (If neither a grinder nor a processor is available, knead all the ingredients by hand. Knead at least twice, adding some of the water to keep the mixture soft and pliable.)

Form the mixture into a large, flattened, pancakelike shape. Spoon melted butter over the *Kibby* when serving.

SERVES 6.

*Note:* If cooked meat is preferred, the ground lamb may be broiled briefly in a skillet as you would any ground meat. Allow the meat to cool and then add to the drained wheat along with the other ingredients.

# Liver Kabobs

1½ pounds liver, calf's or lamb's, cut into 1-inch cubes
12 small white onions
3 medium-sized ripe tomatoes, cut into quarters
2 large green peppers, cut into strips
2 tablespoons salad oil (optional)
¼ teaspoon pepper
½ teaspoon thyme
¼ teaspoon mint, dried
¼ teaspoon allspice
1 teaspoon salt

Put cubed liver, onions, quartered tomatoes, and folded strips of green peppers onto four skewers. If desired, the liver cubes may be rubbed with oil before placing them on the skewers.

In a mixing bowl, combine the pepper, thyme, mint, allspice, and salt, then spread the seasonings on a flat dish. Roll the meat and the other ingredients on the skewers in the spice mixture. Cook over an open fire or in a preheated oven set to high-broil. Broil 3 inches from the flame and 3 minutes per side. Be careful not to overcook.

SERVES 4.

# Lamb-Carrot Casserole

2 pounds boneless lamb, leg or shoulder, cut into
   1-inch cubes
3 tablespoons butter
6 large carrots, sliced
2 medium-sized onions, quartered
1½ cups water
1 teaspoon salt
¾ teaspoon pepper
½ teaspoon ground cloves

Preheat the oven to 350°F. Melt the butter in a pot and brown the meat on all sides. Remove and set aside. Put the carrots, onions, and water in the pot; add the salt, pepper, and cloves. Stir and bring to a boil. When the carrots and onions are tender but firm, combine with the meat in a casserole. Bake approximately 30 minutes.

SERVES 4 TO 5.

*Serve with black olives and slices of mild cheese, such as mozzarella or bland meunster.*

# Lamb with Green Beans

    5 to 6 pounds boned lamb shoulder, cut into 1-inch
        cubes
    2 tablespoons butter
    1 large onion, minced
    1½ cups water
    2 pounds fresh green beans
    1 to 1¼ pounds canned tomatoes, cut into small pieces
    1 teaspoon pepper
    ½ teaspoon cinnamon
    1¼ teaspoons salt

Melt the butter in a pot. Add the meat and onion and brown over a medium heat. Add the water and simmer for 10 minutes. Combine the green beans, tomatoes, and spices with the meat. Simmer over a low heat for 30 minutes.
SERVES 6.

# Persian Baked Lamb
*(Tas Kabab)*

>    1½ pounds lamb, leg or shoulder
>    2 large potatoes
>    2 large onions
>    3 large tomatoes
>    1 teaspoon salt
>    1 teaspoon pepper
>    ¾ teaspoon cinnamon
>    1 teaspoon oregano
>    ½ teaspoon nutmeg
>    2 tablespoons butter
>    ½ cup water

Preheat the oven to 350°F. Cut the lamb into slices ¼ to ½ inch thick. Then cut the slices into pieces about 1½ inches long and 1 inch wide. Peel the potatoes; slice approximately ⅛ inch thick. Slice the onions a fraction thinner. Slice the tomatoes approximately ⅛ inch thick. In small mixing bowl, thoroughly mix the salt, pepper, and spices. Soften the butter.

Add layers of onions, potatoes, meat, and tomatoes to a pot in that order, then sprinkle well with the seasoning mixture. Repeat until all ingredients are used, finishing with a layer of potatoes on top.

Spread the softened butter over the top layer of potatoes. Add the water, trickling it around the inner edges of the pot to allow it to run down. Cover and bake for ½ hour. Remove the cover and bake for an additional 15 minutes.

SERVES 4.

*Slices of chilled cucumber seasoned with salt and pepper make a simple accompaniment to* Tas Kabab.

# Lebanese Leg of Lamb

Feasts and festivals are a frequent part of Lebanese and Syrian life. They are a time for large families living apart to come together. The patriarch of the family purchases a live lamb from the market and fattens it for a week on malt and mulberry leaves. Neighbors and friends join in for the slaughtering of the lamb and to applaud the dressing and seasoning.

In this recipe, the leg of lamb can be roasted either in the traditional way, on a spit, or in the oven.

> 1 leg of lamb (about 5 to 6 pounds)
> 3 cloves garlic, minced
> 1 teaspoon salt
> ½ teaspoon pepper
> ½ teaspoon sage
> ½ teaspoon thyme
> 1 bay leaf, crumbled
> ½ teaspoon marjoram
> 1 teaspoon ground ginger
> 2 tablespoons olive oil
> 10 to 12 small or 6 large (quartered) potatoes, peeled
> 16 small white onions

Have the butcher cut small, ¼-inch gashes on the top of the leg of lamb. Dampen the lamb with a cloth or paper towel. In a mixing bowl, combine the minced garlic, salt, and all the other spices and herbs. Mix thoroughly, then rub all over the top of the leg, filling all the gashes. Rub the remainder of the mixture over the rest of the leg. Brush on a coating of olive oil.

*To roast in the oven:* Preheat the oven to 500°F. Sear the lamb in a 500°F oven for 15 minutes. Reduce the heat to 350°F and roast for approximately 1½ hours. Forty-five minutes before the lamb is done, add the peeled potatoes and onions to the roasting pan. Serve in casserole dish with the lamb.

*To roast over an open fire:* Secure the leg on a roasting spit and roast over a hot fire, turning often. Baste with hot fat drippings. Do not use potatoes and onions for this method of cooking. Roast for approximately 1½ hours.

SERVES 6.

*Serve whole on a platter surrounded by nectarines, pears, apple slices, plums, and grapes.*

# Lamb with Mushrooms

        2 pounds boneless lamb, cut into 1-inch cubes
        6 tablespoons butter
        1 large onion, minced
    1½ teaspoons salt
        1 teaspoon cinnamon
        1 teaspoon pepper
        1 cup water
        4 tablespoons lemon juice
        2 pounds mushrooms, sliced
        3 tablespoons cream sherry
        2 egg yolks

In a pot, melt half of the butter. Add the onion, meat, and seasonings and sauté until browned. Add the water and half of the lemon juice. Stir and simmer for 20 minutes.

In another pan, sauté the mushrooms in the rest of the butter. Add the sautéed mushrooms with the sherry to the pot containing the meat. Stir and simmer for another 15 to 20 minutes or until the meat is tender.

Beat the egg yolks with the remainder of the lemon juice. Add to the pot when ready to serve. Stir and serve over bed of rice.

SERVES 6.

# Lambburgers with Pine Nuts

> 1 pound lamb, leg or shoulder, ground
> ½ to ¾ cup pine nuts
> 1 tablespoon butter
> 1 small onion, minced
> 2 tablespoons parsley, chopped
> ¾ teaspoon mint, dried
> ½ teaspoon salt
> ¼ teaspoon pepper
> 1 can (15 ounces) tomato purée

Preheat the oven to 350°F. Brown the pine nuts in the butter. Set aside. Mix the lamb, onion, parsley, mint, salt, and pepper and shape into hamburger patties with a hollow in the center of each. Fill each hollow with the browned pine nuts and close over. Place the filled lambburgers in a baking pan. Pour tomato purée over the patties. Bake 7 minutes, turn over, and bake another 7 minutes.

SERVES 4.

*Serve with french-fried potatoes and salad.*

# Lady's Thighs Kofte
## (*Kadin Budu Kofte*)

Middle Eastern poets have always been floridly expressive of the female form, at various times describing their loves as having "breasts soft as a doe's eyes," "perspiration sweeter than rose water," and "a waist so slender it seemed but a hair." Little wonder, then, that the cooks, those poets of the palate, would not be outdone, as in this variation of *kofte*—the Turkish term for ground meat.

1¼ pounds lamb, breast or shoulder, ground three times
1 medium-sized onion, chopped
4½ tablespoons butter
1½ teaspoons coarse salt
2½ tablespoons rice
¾ cup dry sherry
3 tablespoons cheese (any of the white or soft cheeses or cottage, feta, farmer's, ricotta, or goat's cheese)
4 eggs, beaten
½ bunch parsley

Sauté the onion in 1 tablespoon of the butter in a pot until transparent. Do not brown. Add the salt, rice, and sherry. Cover and cook until the rice is tender (approximately 30 minutes). Remove the pot from the heat and set aside. In a large, deep skillet, cook the lamb in 1 tablespoonful of the butter. When all juices and butter are extracted, drain the meat and remove from the heat.

Add the rice to the meat. Then add the cheese and knead everything together for five minutes. Shape the mixture into elongated, slightly rounded ovals (in the shape of you know what).

Roll the patties in the beaten eggs and sauté in the remaining 2½ tablespoons of butter until well browned. Serve with sprigs of parsley.

SERVES 6.

# Meatballs Tabriz

The *Khvatay Namak*, or the *Book of Lords*, was written first in Persian, then translated into Arabic in the eighth century. It contains much of the epic material of Middle Eastern folk wisdom—such as, "Music and singing are the necessary attributes of a feast." The book also tells of women dancing to the sound of music, so that the King's "soul shall not be clouded."

Ordinary dishes made unusual also tend to uncloud the soul, as with these meatballs from Tabriz, the capital of Azerbaijan.

Tabriz meatballs are large. The following recipe is designed for 3 large meatballs.

> 2 pounds lamb or beef (chuck or round), ground twice
> ¾ cup yellow split peas
> 3½ cups water
> 1 medium-sized onion, grated
> 1 large egg
> 1 teaspoon lemon juice
> 1 teaspoon salt
> ¾ teaspoon pepper
> ½ teaspoon cinnamon
> ¾ teaspoon saffron
> ½ teaspoon nutmeg
> 9 dried prunes

Preheat the oven to 350°F. Cook the split peas in 3 cups of the water for 30 to 40 minutes. Put the meat into a large mixing bowl. Add the onion, egg, lemon juice, and seasonings and mix well. Drain the split peas, mash them, and add to the meat mixture.

Mix thoroughly, then make 3 large meatballs. Put 3 dried

prunes into the center of each meatball. Place the meatballs in a greased pan with the remaining ½ cup of water. Bake for 30 to 40 minutes.

SERVES 3 TO 6.

*Serve each giant meatball surrounded with a ring of peas.*

# Circassian Chicken

Now part of Russia, Circassia once lay along the Turkish-Russian border and the Caucasus Mountains. Since classical times, Circassia has been known as the land that was "a mountain of languages" because more separate languages are spoken there, in a smaller area, than anywhere else in the world.

There are many recipes for Circassian chicken; here is one of them.

1 roasting chicken (4 to 5 pounds)
2 large onions, quartered
2 medium-sized carrots, cut into quarters
2 stalks celery
8 cups water
1 teaspoon salt
1 teaspoon pepper
1 bay leaf
1 teaspoon chervil
¾ teaspoon basil
1¼ teaspoons sage
1 cup walnuts, shelled
2 small white onions, finely minced
2 cups bread crumbs
¾ tablespoon paprika
1 cup chicken stock (from cooking the chicken)
4 medium eggs
¼ to ½ pound butter

Remove all the innards of the chicken. Put the chicken in a large pot and add the quartered onions, carrots, celery, and water. Add the salt, pepper, bay leaf, chervil, basil, and sage. Stir and bring the water to a boil. Skim any fat from the top of the water and reduce the heat at once. Simmer the chicken for 2½ hours.

Remove the chicken. Strain the stock, and set aside. Let

the chicken cool. Then take off the skin, remove all the meat from the bones in small pieces, almost shredded, and set aside.

Pound the walnuts with a mortar and pestle or splinter in a food processor. When the walnuts are reduced almost to crumbs, add the finely minced white onions, ½ cup of the bread crumbs, and the paprika. Mix thoroughly. Slowly add 1 cup of the strained chicken stock, mixing the walnut mixture to the consistency of a paste.

Mix in 1 unbeaten egg and put aside for 20 minutes, then mix in the shredded pieces of chicken. Form the mixture into cutlets. Beat the remaining 3 eggs and mix with the rest of the bread crumbs. Dip the cutlets into the egg mixture, coating thoroughly. Sauté in butter until lightly browned on both sides.

SERVES 6.

*Serve with green beans or asparagus on the side.*

# Chicken Yogurt Curry

> 1 chicken (3 to 4 pounds), cut up
> 3 cups water
> 1 large stalk celery
> 2 teaspoons salt
> 1½ teaspoons pepper
> 1 quart yogurt
> 1 large egg
> 1 medium-sized onion, chopped
> ½ teaspoon allspice
> 1½ teaspoons curry powder
> 1 tablespoon flour
> 3 tablespoons butter

In a kettle, place the water, chicken, celery stalk, 1 teaspoon of the salt, and ½ teaspoon of the pepper. Simmer, covered, for approximately 1 hour, or until done. Remove from the heat. Pour off the broth and discard the celery stalk. When the chicken is cool enough to handle, discard the skin and bones. Cut the meat into strips or irregular pieces and set aside.

In a double boiler, put the yogurt, egg, onion, allspice, curry powder, and the remainder of the salt and pepper. Over a *low* heat, add the flour gradually and stir until the mixture thickens, approximately 6 minutes. Do not curdle the yogurt. Add the chicken pieces and butter and stir constantly until the butter is dissolved. Cook for another 6 minutes over a low heat.

SERVES 4.

*Serve over toast or rice with a side dish of peas.*

# Chicken Alexandria

1 chicken (3 to 4 pounds), cut into serving-size pieces
2 sticks butter
1 clove garlic, minced
  Juice and rind of 2 lemons
½ teaspoon salt
½ teaspoon pepper
½ teaspoon tarragon

Preheat the oven to 350°F. Place the chicken in a large, shallow oven-proof dish or in a baking pan. Leave enough room for turning the pieces. In a separate pot, melt 1½ sticks of the butter. Grate the rind of the lemons. Add the minced garlic, grated lemon rind, salt, pepper, and tarragon. Mix thoroughly and pour over the chicken pieces. Marinate the chicken for 1 hour in the refrigerator, turning at least once.

Butter generously an earthenware or other cooking dish with the remaining ½ stick of butter. Place the marinated chicken pieces into cooking dish and bake for ¾ to 1 hour or until tender. Baste frequently with the marinade mixture.

Squeeze ½ cup of lemon juice from the remains of the 2 lemons. Ten minutes before serving, add the lemon juice to the chicken. Baste once more with marinade and finish cooking. Serve the chicken hot directly from baking dish with asparagus on the side.

SERVES 4.

*A Chablis is an excellent accompaniment.*

# 2

# THE MEDITERRANEAN LANDS

ANCIENT Greece was composed of independent city-states: Corinth, Sparta, Rhodes, Athens. They competed for trade with all the lands bordering the Mediterranean. As a result, herbs, spices, and culinary innovations were brought to the Hellenic cultures. Every new way of cooking became a source of inspiration to the active, questing classical Greek mind. Everything brought in was refined and adapted.

In the Hellenic states, beef, pork, poultry, calf, sheep, and hare were frequent table meats. The present-day widespread use of lamb in Greece is a heritage of recent centuries. Our knowledge of ancient Greek recipes comes to us from the conquering Romans, who embraced all the Greek dishes with enthusiasm and passed them on to posterity, adding their own touches, of course. The political patterns were paralleled in the kitchen. The roots of today's Italian cuisine are Roman and Greek. The Italian city-states of Naples, Genoa, Florence, Palermo, and Venice were modeled on the Greek city-states, and the Roman use of olives, figs, honey, tomatoes, and spices grew out of the Greek use of those elements.

But the Romans were conquerors more than traders. They returned to Rome more varieties of meats, flavorings, and recipes than the Greek merchants ever brought back to their states. The Roman sophistication in the cooking of meat evolved out of the culinary techniques the conquerors brought back. When Rome was the most powerful force in all her glory, her cuisine reflected that eminence. Veal, beef, game birds, poultry, and pork were served with an opulence befitting Roman culture. The profuse use of condiments, herbs, spices, honey, lemon, figs, and olives was often a means to make palatable meat that was less than tender. But the Romans began to use seasonings to enhance rather than mask the taste of food.

The use of olives and olive oil in Italian cuisine dates back to Roman times. The olive tree can thrive where no other tree can exist, and so olives became a mainstay of Roman cuisine. The modern Italian gastronomic fascination with little songbirds—thrushes, woodpigeons, skylarks, doves, and fig-peckers—also dates back to Roman times. When Imperial Rome was the center of the civilized world, its culinary refinement was unmatched.

The spirit of the Renaissance, culturally and intellectually, was Italian, only fitting as the Italians inherited the knowledge of Rome. The monks contributed much to the emergence of good cooking once again. As the Renaissance spread across all of Europe, the Italian ways with meat also penetrated other European countries, especially France. When Catherine de Medici came to France to marry Henry II, she brought chefs who taught the refinements of Italian cooking. They introduced new ways of cooking meat as well as new cuts and special dishes—such as *tournedos*, which have become known as *medaillons de veau; quenelles* of chicken; and a round *torte* made of ham, cheese, and chestnuts, possibly the father of the French *quiche*.

Once again, meat became a food to enjoy and to savor, instead of simply to eat. Non-Italians today speak of Italian cooking, but Italians speak of Genoese cooking; the veal of Lombardy; beef in Tuscany; the *agnello* (lamb) in the Roman manner; the pork of Sardinia and hams of Parma; and the great dishes and cuisines of Venice, Verona, and Sicily, where the influence of the Moors is still apparent in the cuisine.

Our museums are filled with objects from ancient Greece and Rome, and at our tables we enjoy other testimonials to those cultures: *Veal Rollatine, Saltimbocca, Maialino Arrostito, Agnellino, Torta de ricotta, Stiphato,* and *Souvlakia,* to name but a few. The infinite variety of ways to serve meat, game, and poultry is largely a Mediterranean inheritance, a gift that has survived through the centuries. These dishes are not the gift of a great chef or even of a particular school or style of planned cuisine; they have evolved out of the life-styles of the Mediterranean basin, its social and political turmoil. They are indeed a monument of the table for all to enjoy.

# Stifatho

*Stifatho* is the Greek word for stew. This recipe for a Greek ragout was supposedly very popular in ancient Athens.

    2 pounds beef chuck, cut into 1-inch cubes
    ½ cup salad oil
    3 cloves garlic, minced
    1 large onion, chopped
    ½ teaspoon salt
    ¼ teaspoon pepper
    1½ pounds small white onions
    1 cup tomato purée or paste
    ¼ teaspoon basil
    ¼ teaspoon thyme
    ¼ teaspoon oregano
    1 glass (about ½ cup) dry red wine
    2 bay leaves

Heat the oil in a large pot. Add the meat, garlic, chopped onion, salt, and pepper. Brown the meat on all sides, then add the small whole onions.

Season the tomato purée with the basil, thyme, and oregano and mix well. Add the seasoned tomato purée to the pot, followed by the wine and bay leaves. Cover and simmer slowly over a low heat for 1 hour. Remove the bay leaves and simmer for approximately 1¼ hours longer or until the meat is tender. Remove the cover and cook until the sauce is reduced to the consistency of a thick jam.

Serves 4.

*Serve hot with a Greek wine, a salad, and rolls.*

# Ragout Pebronata

Cookery has been described as an "art connected with civilized life." Even the rough-hewn Corsican peasants agreed with that definition, as demonstrated by this recipe for stew with a special sauce.

>     2 pounds beef top rump or flank, diced into 1-inch
>         pieces
>     2 tablespoons olive oil
>     ½ teaspoon pepper
>     ½ teaspoon basil
>     ¼ teaspoon marjoram
>     ¼ teaspoon dill weed
>     ½ cup white wine

*Pebronata Sauce*

>     4 medium-sized green peppers
>     5 tablespoons olive oil
>     1 small onion, chopped
>     2 cloves garlic, chopped
>     ½ cup parsley, chopped
>     ½ teaspoon thyme
>     1 pound ripe tomatoes
>     9 juniper berries, crushed
>     1 large onion, sliced
>     1 tablespoon flour
>     1 cup full-bodied red wine

Brown the meat evenly on all sides in the oil in a large pot. Add the pepper, basil, marjoram, and dill to the white wine. Stir thoroughly and pour over the browned meat. Cover and simmer for approximately 2 hours.

To prepare the Pebronata Sauce, discard the core and seeds of the green peppers. Slice them into strips approximately 1 inch long and ⅛ to ¼ inch wide and set aside. Heat 2 tablespoons of the olive oil in a skillet and stir in chopped onion, garlic, parsley, and thyme. Cook over a low heat for 5 minutes. Chop the tomatoes in eighths and add to the skillet along with the juniper berries. Simmer for 20 minutes.

In a separate skillet, simmer the sliced onion in the remaining olive oil until yellow and softened. Add the green pepper slices and simmer until softened. Stir in the flour and then add the red wine. Stir well and cook over a moderate heat until the wine is reduced by two-thirds.

Strain the tomato sauce through a sieve and then add to the skillet containing the green peppers and wine. Cook over a low heat for 5 minutes longer.

Add the Pebronata Sauce to the meat 15 minutes before the meat is finished and serve together.

SERVES 4.

*A simple salad and rolls can be a good accompaniment.*

# Steak Sautéed in Wine and Brandy

Nola, a small city near Naples, annually celebrates its feast of *Gigli di Nola*, or Lilies of Nola. The festivities are supported by the seven town guilds, and their emblems are boldly displayed—sometimes made of papier-mâché, sometimes carved, sometimes of sugar and marzipan. There is a waistcoat for the tailors, a last for the shoemakers, an anvil for the blacksmiths, a flask of wine and a piece of cheese for the grocers, a loaf of bread for the bakers, a sheaf of wheat for the farmers, and a horned ox head for the butchers.

    4 beef fillet or shell steaks, 1 to 1¼ inches thick
    ½ teaspoon salt
    ½ teaspoon pepper
    2 tablespoons olive oil
    3 tablespoons butter
    ½ cup chopped liver pâté
    ¼ cup Marsala wine
    ⅓ cup brandy

Mix the salt and pepper together and sprinkle on the steaks. Rub both sides of the steaks with olive oil and set aside for 1 hour. Grill the steaks over a high heat for two minutes on each side.

In a skillet large enough to hold the steaks, melt the butter, add the chopped liver pâté, and cook to a thick purée. When thickened, add the Marsala wine. Cook for 2 minutes more and then add the grilled steaks.

Turn the steaks once to coat both sides with the sauce. Pour the brandy over the steaks, light, and let burn. When the flames die out, the steaks are ready to serve.

SERVES 4.

*Mixed green vegetables served separately and a good burgundy accompany this dish well.*

# Meat Sauce
*(Salsa Con Carne)*

        1 pound beef chuck, ground
        1 large onion, chopped
        2 cloves garlic, chopped
        2 tablespoons olive oil
        1 can (8 ounces) tomato paste
        2 mushrooms, finely chopped
        1 teaspoon parsley, finely chopped
        ½ stalk celery, finely chopped
        ½ teaspoon salt
        ¼ teaspoon Tabasco sauce
        ¼ teaspoon Worcestershire sauce
        ½ teaspoon pepper
        ½ teaspoon basil
        ½ teaspoon oregano
        ½ teaspoon rosemary
        1 bay leaf
        2 cups warm water

Brown the onions and garlic in the olive oil in a saucepan. Add the meat and brown evenly. Stir in the tomato paste and simmer for 5 minutes. Add all the other ingredients and mix thoroughly. Simmer, stirring, for at least 2 minutes. Then cover and simmer for 45 minutes to 1 hour. Remove the bay leaf and simmer for an additional 15 minutes. If the sauce becomes too thick, add a little more water, but only a little.

SERVES 4.

*Serve with pasta or rice.*

# Fresh Tongue with Mushroom Marinade

2 fresh calf's tongues (not smoked or pickled), about
   1½ pounds each
10 to 12 mushrooms, thinly sliced
½ cup orange brandy
   Water
½ cup flour
3 tablespoons salad oil
4 stalks celery, finely chopped
4 medium-sized yellow onions, finely chopped
1 green pepper, finely chopped
¼ teaspoon salt
¼ teaspoon pepper
1 tablespoon grated orange rind
2 tablespoons cognac

Combine the thinly sliced mushrooms with the orange brandy in a deep dish and marinate overnight. Place the tongues in a pot of boiling water. Cover and boil for 1½ hours. Remove the tongues, cool slightly, and peel away the thin, white outer layer of the skin. Place the tongues on a cutting board and slice lengthwise in ¼-inch-wide slices. Lightly flour one side of the tongue slices and place on a flat dish or waxed paper.

In a large pan, heat oil to bubbling. Add the celery, onions, and green pepper and sauté until softened. Add the salt and pepper and mix. Then add the grated orange rind and mix again. Add the cognac and stir well as it sizzles. Put the tongue slices into the pan, lower the flame at once, and let simmer, covered, for 30 minutes. Remove the cover and stir. Then cover again and simmer for 10 minutes more.

Drain the mushrooms that have marinated overnight. In a separate saucepan, warm the mushrooms in the marinade and then drain. Discard the marinade. Spoon the mushrooms over the tongue when it is served.

SERVES 4.

*Serve the tongue over a flat layer of rice, along with gravy from the pan in which the tongue was cooked. Buttered string beans and endive salad go well with this dish, along with a full-bodied white wine.*

# Roast Leg of Veal

The ancient Egyptians and Hebrews knew the pleasure of veal, but until centuries later, it was considered a special occasion dish. Social, political, and religious factors worked against veal for ordinary table use. The pre-Renaissance Tuscan merchant, Francesco di Marco Datini, aided the resurgence of veal by quoting his doctor, "Place it in your belly, in every way you can, for you can have no more wholesome victuals."

> 1 leg of veal (3 to 4 pounds)
> 2 slices bacon
> 2 large onions, finely chopped
> ½ cup white wine
> 3 tablespoons salad oil
> 1 tablespoon bread crumbs
> 1 teaspoon chives, finely chopped
> 2 cloves garlic, mashed
> 1 teaspoon salt
> ½ teaspoon pepper
> 2 anchovies, puréed
> 1 tablespoon Parmesan cheese, grated

Preheat the oven to 300°F. Fry the bacon strips. Cool and pulverize them. Set aside. On the bottom of a baking pan, place the chopped onions and wine. Place the leg of veal on a rack in the baking pan. Bake for 45 minutes. Remove from the oven and let cool.

In a bowl, place the bacon, salad oil, bread crumbs, chives, garlic, salt, pepper, puréed anchovies, and grated cheese. Mix together thoroughly. Pat the veal dry and rub the mixture generously all over the meat. If any of mixture is left over, mix it into the liquid in the bottom of the baking pan. Raise the oven to 325°F.

Place the leg of veal back on the rack in the pan and continue baking for ½ hour longer. Use liquid in pan as gravy.

SERVES 6 TO 8.

*Serve hot with mixed vegetables and a cold Chablis.*

# Veal Chops Palermitana

    4 veal chops, rib or loin
    ¼ teaspoon salt
    ¼ teaspoon pepper
    1 tablespoon salad oil
    1 avocado, peeled and cut into quarters
    6 cloves garlic
    1 teaspoon chives
    ½ cup heavy cream
    2 tablespoons horseradish

Preheat the oven to 350°F. Rub the veal chops with salt, pepper, and oil. In an oven-proof dish, bake for ½ hour.

In a blender or food processor, put the avocado, garlic, chives, cream, and horseradish and blend thoroughly. (If blender or processor is unavailable, mash the avocado into a purée, then mix thoroughly by hand with other ingredients.) Put the mixture into a saucepan, heat, and serve over the veal chops.

SERVES 2 TO 4.

*This mixture can also be used over cold meats. Do not heat.*

# Veal Chops with Olives

5 veal chops, loin or rib
5 tablespoons butter
½ cup ham, finely diced
1 medium-sized onion, chopped
¼ teaspoon dry mustard
½ cup green olives, pitted and coarsely chopped

Melt the butter in a skillet. Fry the chops on both sides until golden brown, approximately 8 to 10 minutes on each side. Remove the chops from the skillet. Add the onion, mustard, and diced ham to the skillet and stir well for 5 minutes over a low heat. Put the veal chops back in the skillet, cover, and cook over a low heat for 10 minutes. Turn the chops and cook 10 minutes longer.

Transfer the chops to a heated platter or keep warm in the oven. Add the chopped olives to the skillet, stir, and heat. Pour the sauce over the chops.

SERVES 5.

*Serve with buttered noodles and a dark beer or ale.*

# Spiced Veal Burgers

        1 pound veal shoulder, ground
        ¾ teaspoon salt
        ¼ teaspoon ground cumin
        ½ teaspoon oregano
        2 tablespoons butter or margarine
        2 tablespoons salad oil
        1 medium-sized zucchini, cut into ¼-inch cubes
        ½ cup Parmesan cheese, grated

Mix the veal well with ¼ teaspoon of the salt, cumin, and oregano. In a large frying pan, melt butter or margarine and oil and add the remaining salt. Put in the cubed zucchini, mix well, and cook for 10 minutes. Mix again, shape into patties, and then put veal burgers into pan. Cook for 5 minutes, turn the burgers, sprinkle with cheese, cover, and cook for 5 minutes more.

Makes 5 burgers.

*Serve over rice. Tossed salad and a white wine make good accompaniments.*

# Lamb Feta

1½ pounds boneless lamb shoulder, cut into ¼- to
½-inch cubes
½ to ¾ pound lamb bones
3 tablespoons salad oil
1 large onion, finely chopped
½ teaspoon marjoram
½ teaspoon salt
¼ teaspoon pepper
5 cloves garlic, crushed
12 black olives, pitted and cut into quarters
2 cups rice, uncooked
2 cups chicken bouillon or stock
1 large egg, beaten
½ pound feta cheese

Heat the oil in a large pot. Add the onion and sauté until soft. Add the marjoram, salt, pepper, garlic, and olives. Mix thoroughly, then add the lamb meat and bones. Cover and cook for 1 hour over a low heat. Stir three or four times during cooking.

When the meat is almost ready, cook the rice in the chicken bouillon for about ½ hour. When the meat is done, remove and discard the bones. Crumble the feta cheese and add to the beaten egg. Mix and stir into the rice for a minute and spread over a serving plate. From the pot, pour the lamb and sauce over the feta-rice mixture.

SERVES 4 TO 5.

*Serve with ½ breaded tomato per person, buttered spinach, and a rosé wine.*

# Lamb Shanks Aegean

In ancient Greece, thyme was a symbol of bravery and sacrifice. It was thought to impart vigor and energy. To tell someone that he "smelled of thyme" was a great compliment. Roman officers used to bathe in thyme-sprinkled water to gain strength and courage. A dish such as this satisfied the stomach and the psyche.

    4 lamb shanks, cracked
    ½ cup salad oil
    ¼ teaspoon salt
    ¼ teaspoon pepper
    ½ teaspoon thyme
    ¼ teaspoon basil
    ½ teaspoon fresh dill weed, chopped
    ½ cup red wine
    2 green peppers, cut up
    12 small white onions (whole)
    12 cherry tomatoes (whole)
    24 black olives, pitted and halved
    12 mushrooms (caps only), sliced

In a large pot, heat the oil and add the salt, pepper, thyme, basil, and dill. Mix well and add the lamb shanks. Brown the shanks, then pour in the wine. Stir thoroughly and turn the shanks. Add the green peppers and onions, cover, and cook for 1 hour at 350°F. (Use a thermometer to measure the temperature.)

Turn the shanks, add the tomatoes and black olives, and cook for ½ hour longer. Add the mushrooms, stir, and turn the shanks. Cook, uncovered, for another 20 minutes.

SERVES 4.

*Serve with biscuits or rice, red wine, and green salad.*

# Lamb Chops con Formaggio

   6 shoulder lamb chops, 1 inch thick
   ½ tablespoon salt
   ½ teaspoon pepper
   1 tablespoon dry mustard
   1 teaspoon oregano
   2 cloves garlic, crushed
   3 tablespoons tomato paste
   1 large green pepper, coarsely chopped
   1 large onion, sliced into rings and separated
   3 tomatoes, cut into ¼-inch round slices
   ½ cup Parmesan or Romano cheese, grated

Preheat the oven to 350°F. Mix the salt, pepper, dry mustard, oregano, and garlic. Arrange the chops in an oven-proof baking dish. Sprinkle the chops thoroughly with the seasoning mixture. Spread the tomato paste over the chops and sprinkle evenly with green peppers. Place the onion rings over the peppers on each chop and put tomato slices on top.

Bake for 45 minutes. Then sprinkle grated cheese evenly over all the chops. Lower the oven to 300°F and bake 15 minutes longer.

SERVES 3 TO 6.

# Carnival Lamb

Our word *carnival* comes from the Latin *carne vale*, which means "farewell to meat" and once signified only the period before Lent. That time was devoted to feasting, special meat dishes, and merrymaking in anticipation of the period of fasting and self-discipline.

    1 leg of lamb, boned (6–7 pounds)
    ¾ pound spinach, chopped
    2 apples
    5 slices soft cheese, such as Jarlsberg
    2 tablespoons bread crumbs, seasoned
    ¼ teaspoon ginger
    ½ teaspoon dry mustard
    ¼ teaspoon thyme
    ¼ stick butter, melted
    Apple brandy

Preheat the oven to 325°F. Cook the spinach until it is half-done and set aside.

Peel both apples, keeping the skin in long circular sections. Set the skin aside and cut the apples into small pieces. Place the pieces on the bottom of a baking pan.

Open up the boned leg of lamb to lie flat. Spread the spinach over the lamb. Place slices of cheese over the spinach and sprinkle with the bread crumbs. Mix the ginger, mustard, and thyme and sprinkle over all. Pour the melted butter over everything.

Roll the lamb and tuck in ends. Tie it crisscross to secure the stuffing inside. As an added touch, the apple rind can be rolled around the lamb. Place the lamb on a rack and put the rack in the pan lined with the apples. Bake for 1½ hours. When ready to serve, flame at the table with a thin coating of apple brandy.

SERVES 6.

*Serve with cinnamon-applesauce and a chilled Sauterne.*

# Meat Loaf Bolognese

The Bolognese are famous for combining different kinds of meats in one dish or stuffing. In their *Tortellini*, traditionally served on Christmas Eve, the stuffing is made of pork, veal, ham, turkey breast, sausage, cheese, veal brains, eggs, nutmeg, butter, salt, and pepper.

    1 pound pork
    1 pound veal
    ½ pound ham
    ½ pound bacon
    2 medium-sized onions, minced
    1 tablespoon parsley, chopped
    1 can (4 ounces) tomato sauce
    ¼ teaspoon oregano
    3 tablespoons bread crumbs
    1 cup beer
    2 egg whites
    2 tablespoons Parmesan cheese, grated

Have all the meat ground together twice. Preheat the oven to 350°F. Mix the ground meat with the onions, parsley, tomato sauce, oregano, bread crumbs, and beer into a large mixing bowl. Mix thoroughly. Turn the seasoned meat into a loaf pan and bake for 30 minutes.

Blend the egg whites and Parmesan cheese. Beat together with an eggbeater until smooth. Remove the loaf from the oven, spread the cheese-egg mixture over the top of the loaf, and return to the oven. Bake for another 20 minutes.

SERVES 6.

# Chicken Marsala

1 frying or roasting chicken (approximately 4 pounds),
    cut into serving-size pieces
1 small eggplant, unpeeled and cut into 1-inch squares
1 teaspoon salt
¼ teaspoon pepper
2 tablespoons butter
1 medium-sized onion, sliced
1 clove garlic, chopped
½ teaspoon marjoram
¾ cup Marsala wine
¼ cup hot water

Sprinkle the eggplant with ¼ teaspoon of the salt and set aside for ½ to 1 hour. Rub the remaining salt and pepper over the outside of the chicken. Melt the butter in a skillet, add the chicken, and brown on both sides. Add the onion, garlic, and marjoram. Pour in the Marsala wine, stir, and reduce the heat. Let the Marsala bubble until it is reduced by one-third. Add the water and reduce the heat. Simmer, covered, for 20 to 30 minutes or until tender. After ten minutes of cooking, add the eggplant and stir. If necessary, add a little more water.

SERVES 4.

*String beans cooked in butter and lemon juice go well with this dish. Sauté an onion in creamed butter sauce and serve on top of the string beans.*

# Chicken with Ham and Fennel

Fennel (*finocchio* in Italian) was considered, because of its sweet agreeableness, a symbol of flattery by sixteenth-century Italians. The colloquial expression *dare finocchio* meant to give fennel, to flatter someone.

> 1 frying or roasting chicken (3 to 4 pounds)
> ½ pound ham, sliced into slivers
> ¼ teaspoon pepper
> ½ teaspoon fennel
> 2 cloves garlic
> 3 tablespoons butter

Have the chicken cleaned. Stuff with the slivers of ham, cutting any that are too long to fit comfortably. Mix the pepper and fennel and sprinkle inside the chicken, rubbing a little on the outside as well. Insert 2 garlic cloves into the ham stuffing inside the chicken.

Put the butter on the bottom of an oven-proof covered casserole dish and melt it. Place the chicken in the dish, cover, and cook at a moderate heat (400°F) for 20 minutes per pound. (Measure the temperature with a thermometer if exactness is desired.)

SERVES 3 TO 4.

*String beans, buttered and stirred with grated Parmesan cheese, and a good Lambrusco would go well with this dish.*

# Partridges Klephti

The Greek bandits and thieves of the mountains were called Klephtis—a name derived from the Greek word meaning "to steal." From the name *Klephti* came our word *kleptomania*. As the Klephtis were always on the run from the authorities, they developed a method of cooking game birds (and meat) that enabled them to leave on a moment's notice. The partridges, seasoned, were wrapped in paper with fat and whatever vegetables they had and cooked in an earthen pot set over a hole in which a slow fire burned. If they suddenly had to flee, they simply scooped up dinner and took it with them to the next place. The dinner remained flavorful when the cooking was completed.

> 4 partridges (about 1 pound each), cleaned
> 4 sheets aluminum foil
> ½ stick butter
> 16 small white onions
> 2 carrots, diced
> 1 large eggplant, diced
> 1 teaspoon pepper
> 1 teaspoon basil
> 4 bay leaves
> 4 bacon strips

Cut one sheet of aluminum foil for each bird, enough to wrap it completely. Butter the inside of each sheet generously. Place the partridge in the sheet along with 4 onions, ¼ of the carrots, and ¼ of the eggplant. Mix the pepper, basil, and bay leaves together and use ¼ of the mixture to sprinkle over each bird. Place a bacon strip on each bird, wrap in foil, and cook in a 300°F oven for 45 minutes.
SERVES 4.

# Grilled Quail

In Renaissance Italy, heroic or romantic vows were often made at banquets by the lords and nobles assembled. The vow was made in the name of the bird the vowmaker preferred—the vow of the swan, peacock, heron, thrush, dove, pheasant, etc. Usually, the bird named was also the crowning dish of the banquet.

> 6 quail, cleaned but left whole
> 1½ teaspoons salt
> 1½ teaspoons pepper
> 6 slices bacon
> 6 pats butter
> 24 to 30 large mushrooms
> 6 slices bread
> 3 tablespoons butter, softened

Press each bird with a damp towel. Mix the salt and pepper together. Sprinkle each bird with ¼ teaspoon, then rub inside and out with the rest of the seasoning. Lay 1 slice of bacon over and around each quail. Put 1 pat of butter inside each bird.

Cut the stems off the mushrooms and discard. Take two roasting pans. Make a bed of from 4 to 5 mushroom caps for each quail, 3 birds to a pan unless more can fit in comfortably. Place the pans in the broiler under a medium flame (400°F) and broil for 10 to 12 minutes on each side. Baste once or twice with drippings from the pan.

Toast the 6 slices of bread and butter generously with the 3 tablespoons of softened butter. When the quail are done, place each quail, with its mushroom bed, on 1 slice of the buttered toast. Serve hot.

SERVES 6.

*A full-bodied white wine is a must.*

# Rock Cornish Game Hens con Piselli

4 Rock Cornish game hens
3 tablespoons butter
1 large onion, cut into eighths
4 ounces cooked ham, diced
2 ounces cooked tongue, diced
½ teaspoon basil
½ teaspoon pepper
½ teaspoon salt
1 cup white wine
¼ cup chicken stock or broth
1½ pounds fresh green peas

Preheat the oven to 350°F. Melt the butter in a large pan. Brown the onion sections, add the ham and tongue, and simmer for 3 minutes. Add the hens, raise the heat, and brown on all sides. Mix the basil, pepper, and salt and sprinkle the browned hens thoroughly.

Reduce the heat and pour in the wine. When the wine bubbles, pour in the broth. Bake, covered, for 25 minutes. Add the peas and bake 20 minutes longer or until the hens are tender. Add more wine if necessary and baste occasionally.

SERVES 4.

*Serve with buttered halves of toast.*

# Hare Kephallenia

Many ancient peoples attributed mystic powers to hares, some believing that witches changed themselves into hares at will. This recipe comes from the small Ionian island of Kephallenia off the Greek coast. For today's use, rabbit can be substituted for hare.

> 1 hare or rabbit, skinned and cut up
> 1 teaspoon salt
> ½ teaspoon pepper
>    Juice of 6 lemons
> 1 cup olive oil
> 1 large yellow onion, sliced
> ½ tablespoon oregano
> 9 cloves garlic
> 1 cup red wine

A deep, heavy pot is necessary for this dish; earthenware is preferable, although iron, ceramic interior, or copper pots will do. Aluminum should be avoided.

Place the cut-up pieces of rabbit or hare into the pot. Mix ½ teaspoon of the salt and ¼ teaspoon of the pepper together and sprinkle over the meat. Then pour the lemon juice over everything. Let the meat marinate for 6 to 12 hours, 24 hours if possible.

When ready to cook, heat the olive oil in another heavy pot (or remove the meat and thoroughly clean the pot used for the marinade). Add the sliced onion and cook it slightly, then add the meat. Brown the hare or rabbit on both sides. Add the remainder of the salt and pepper, the oregano, and garlic cloves. Stir and mix, then add the wine. Cover the pot and simmer over low heat for 2½ hours or until tender.
SERVES 4.
*Serve with spinach and mushroom salad.*

# 3
# THE BRITISH ISLES

THE English are generally regarded as a nation of beef-eaters. It is an impression once welcomed and fostered by politics more than the palate. When Henry VIII broke with Rome over his divorce of Catherine of Aragon, and France and Spain sided with Rome, he decided to sever all bonds with the Continent—military, political, emotional, and culinary. The fit of royal fury withdrew England into herself, and all things European were rejected. At least that was the official posture, although wealthy friends had no scruples about sneaking in a French dress or an Italian chef whenever they could.

But beef became both patriotic and gastronomically feasible. Fine beef cattle were available for the English table, and the everyday Englishman had never been entirely comfortable with European culinary ways. In any case, the insular nature of English cuisine can be largely laid at the doorstep of the Tudor monarchs.

Although the English rejected sauces and heavy embellishments, they brought the roasting of meat to a fine art. They concentrated attention on the purity of the taste of meat. But it is a misconception that the English were almost exclusively beefeaters. Housekeeping lists of an English manor in the year 1552 reveal that the lord, his family, guests, and servants consumed 4 cows, 29 calves, 14 steers, 54 lambs, 129 sheep, 9 sows, 2 boars, 5 bacon hogs, 3 goats, 7 kids, 13 bucks, 1 stag, and 5 does during the year—a considerably more varied menu than one of just beef.

Walter de la Mare, in his charming book *Come Hither*, cites the "Bill of Fare at the Christening of Mr. Constable's Child" (Mr. Constable being Rector of Cockley Clay in Norfolk). The assembled guests, who apparently constituted the entire village, had the following menu on January 2, 1682:

A whole hog's head souc'd with carrots in the mouth and
   pendents in the ears, with gilded oranges thick sett
2 ox cheeks stewed with 6 marrow bones
A leg of veal larded with 6 pullets

A leg of mutton with 6 rabbits

A chine of beef, chine of venison, chine of mutton, chine
of veal, chine of pork, supported by 4 men

A venison pasty

A great minced pye with 12 small ones about it

A gelt fat turkey with 6 capons

A bustard with 6 pluver

A pheasant with 6 woodcock

A great dish of tarts made with all sweetmeats

A Westphalia hamm with 6 tongues

A jowle of sturgeon

A great charge of all sorts of sweetmeats with wine and all
sorts of liquors answerable

Again, there was a great deal more than simply beef. For those who wonder about the old English terms, a *chine* was the entire backbone with adjoining parts—what we today call the loin, rib, and sirloin. A *gelt* fat turkey was a castrated turkey.

In time, the English began to publish cookbooks, all designed for the English kitchen. Many of these cookbooks discussed manners, etiquette, the treatment of servants, and general deportment as much as they did cooking. Almost all railed against European cooking, especially the French and Italian. In one of the most famous books, Hannah Glasse's *The Art of Cookery*, the author is indignant about the wasteful attitudes of European cooks: "I have heard of a (French) cook that used six pounds of butter to fry twelve eggs!"

Scotland and Ireland felt the culinary influence of the English "withdrawal" from Europe, and they, in turn, influenced English cooking. Much of the fine English beef was bred in Scotland. But Scotland was also a land of dairy cows, and Scottish cooking made heavy use of dough, porridges, and oatmeals. The hills of Scotland were always full of grouse, pheasant, partridge, woodcock, quail, hares, and, of course, deer.

Ireland existed under an English rule which was very harsh in recent centuries. In Ireland, there was no need to fight off European influences; there was time only to fight poverty and English rule. Owning land was forbidden to the Irish, as were most positions of any power or influence. The great estates were all owned by the English or by Irish families with English ties, the Anglo-Irish. As a result, the manor house was the site of great feasts and splendor. The servants and tenant farmers received the shanks, ends, and leftover sections that came down from the big house. Necessity dictated culinary tastes. The tenant farmers had no huge hearth able to roast an entire ox or pig, even if they could come upon such largesse. The iron pot for cooking meat already sectioned came into being as the chief utensil of the kitchen. Stews and pot roasts became the basis of Irish cooking.

The Irish stew remains the father of the true pot roast. The potato was basic to the Irish stew because poverty did not allow for a bounty of vegetables. Corned beef brisket originated with the desire to preserve the good pieces of meat which came into the hands of the tenant farmers. They "corned" the beef, meaning it was preserved in salt. They found that the process not only preserved the meat but also produced a new and tasty flavor. Out of poverty and social restrictions the cuisine of Ireland came into being.

Mutton has always been a much-used meat throughout the British Isles. Much of it was tough and aged, and because they couldn't get the olives, tomatoes, strong herbs, and spices available to the European cook, mutton was boiled for long periods to make it palatable. The meat pie dishes created by English cooks also added flavor and character to the meat with a tasty pastry covering, eggs, potatoes, mushrooms, etc.

It was the English custom, up through the Victorian era, to serve everything belonging to the main meal at one time. The "groaning board" could be taken literally, as tables were weighed down by beef, venison, quail, veal, and pork. A "course" often meant twenty kinds of meat or five kinds of soup.

Dinner in medieval England was taken at midday, but as the social habits of Englishmen changed with the centuries, dinner was gradually advanced to early afternoon. By the eighteenth century, dinner was at four o'clock and by the end of that century, Englishmen were sitting down to dinner at six or seven. However, during all those years, the dinner hour moved back and forth with great argument, and there was much discussion about the proper time to take one's dinner. The controversy grew so widespread, and the adherents of various hours so adamant, that the English essayist Thomas De Quincey felt it necessary to settle matters with a definition of dinner that would at least settle that aspect of the argument. He defined dinner as: "That meal, no matter when taken, which is the principal meal, i.e., the meal on which the day's support is thrown . . . in which meat predominates."

# Roast Beef

With good beef, simple is best for this classic dish. Use the inner seasoning method and season more than just the outer layer of fat.

> 1 rib roast, about a 4-bone roast
> ½ teaspoon salt
> ½ teaspoon freshly ground pepper
> ½ teaspoon dry mustard

Have the butcher cut the top outside layer of fat away but leave a little hinge at one end. Also have the bones cut off. Save the fat and bones.

Preheat the oven to 450°F. Mix the salt, pepper, and dry mustard. Rub the mixture into the meat, then replace the outside layer of fat.

Place the bones in a roasting pan to form a cradle, which will serve as a rack. Put the meat on top of the bones. (When the roast is done you can eat your rack, too.)

Roast the meat, uncovered, for 10 minutes at 450°F. Then reduce the heat to 350°F and continue roasting for 1 hour and 20 minutes for rare, 15 minutes longer for medium, or 30 minutes longer for well done. Baste occasionally.

SERVES 8.

*Serve with a good Bordeaux or Burgundy.*

# Rolled Boneless Rib Roast

1 rib roast, 6–8 pounds
4 large potatoes, cut into large pieces (optional)
3 carrots, cut into large pieces lengthwise and then cut
    into smaller pieces (optional)

Have the butcher bone, roll, and tie the roast. Season and
roast the same as for Roast Beef (p. 85). Use a rack in a
roasting pan or make a bed, which will serve as a rack, of
potatoes and carrots. Do not baste. If a vegetable bed is used,
turn the roast over once.

SERVES 8.

*Serve vegetables along with the roast.*

# Beef and Mushroom Pie

1¼ pounds beef chuck, top round, or sirloin, diced into
    1-inch squares
    Pastry dough (your own or prepared mix)
1 package (10 ounces) frozen peas
1 large onion, finely chopped
¾ stick butter or margarine
½ cup flour
1 cup beef bouillon or brown stock
1½ cups milk
1½ cups mushrooms, sliced
¼ teaspoon salt
¼ teaspoon pepper
1 egg, beaten

Make the pastry dough first. If you are making your own pastry dough, prepare it and set aside (see Pastry Dough for Meat Pies below).

Preheat the oven to 400°F. Cook the peas in a saucepan and set aside. Sauté chopped onion in ½ stick of the butter until it is softened. Add the diced beef and cook for 10 minutes, stirring constantly to brown evenly on all sides. Stir in the flour and cook over a reduced heat, gradually adding the beef bouillon and milk. Bring to a boil and cook, stirring until the mixture becomes smooth.

In a separate pan, sauté the sliced mushrooms in the remaining butter. Add the mushrooms and peas to the meat. Season with salt and pepper and turn into a pie pan or oven-proof casserole. Cover with the pastry dough and brush with the beaten egg. Bake for approximately 30 minutes. The pie should be done when the pastry dough is golden and crisp.

SERVES 4.

*Pastry Dough for Meat Pies*

There are many recipes for pastry dough, prepared pie-crust and pastry mixes. However, since pre-Renaissance times, the English have favored what they call a rough-puff pastry for meat pies, where they prefer a thicker, higher crust. As meat pies are so much a part of English cooking, we include here a recipe for the rough-puff pastry as used in England and elsewhere in the British Isles.

> 2¼ cups all-purpose or self-rising flour
> ¾ teaspoon salt
> 1 cup lard, fat, or vegetable shortening
> ¾ tablespoon lemon juice
> ½ cup water

Sift 2 cups of the flour and the salt together into a large mixing bowl. Cut the lard (or other fat) into small pieces and add to sifted flour. Add the lemon juice and enough water to make the dough semistiff but pliable. Knead the dough-lard mixture with your hands for a few minutes. Sprinkle some of the remaining ¼ cup of flour onto a pastry board. Spread the dough onto a board. Flour a rolling pin and roll out the dough, pressing it into a flat oblong shape.

Fold the dough in three, as though you were folding a sheet of paper to put into an envelope. Press the edges together and roll out again with a rolling pin. Repeat the process one more time. Turn the dough after folding the last time, roll out from the side this time. Set it aside in the refrigerator for 15 to 30 minutes before using.

When covering the meat pie, shape the edges of the dough around a pan or casserole with a little extra thickness or crimp tightly. Leftover pastry dough may be used to form bows, initials, or any other decorative touch on top of the pie.

Makes enough dough for 1 meat pie.

*This dough may be used for any of the meat pies. Do not forget to glaze dough with the beaten egg before putting pie into oven.*

# Steak and Kidney Pie

There are many versions of this classic English dish. We offer two: the first (which follows) is a more elaborate recipe, whereas the second (Birmingham Steak and Kidney Pie) is a simpler one for the traditionalists.

    3 pounds beef sirloin
    1 pound veal kidneys
    2 cups lightly salted water
    1/4 teaspoon salt
    1/2 teaspoon pepper
    4 tablespoons flour
    4 tablespoons butter
    2 medium-sized onions, chopped
    1/2 green pepper, chopped
    1 stalk celery, chopped
    1/2 pound mushrooms, chopped
    1 cup beef bouillon
    1/2 cup port wine
    1 dash cayenne
    Pastry dough (your own or prepared mix)

Have the butcher cut the sirloin into 1-inch cubes and remove all fat from the kidneys. Let the kidneys soak in lightly salted water at least six hours, overnight if possible.

When ready to prepare the meal, dry the kidneys, remove the membranes, and cut into 1/2-inch cubes. Mix the salt and pepper into the flour and dredge the beef and kidney cubes. In a large skillet, melt 2 tablespoons of the butter and brown the meat on all sides. In a separate skillet, melt the remainder of the butter and sauté the onions, pepper, and celery until the onions are golden. Add the chopped mushrooms, reduce the heat, and simmer until the mushrooms are limp.

Combine the vegetables with the meat and add the bouillon, wine, and cayenne. Stir thoroughly. When the mixture bubbles, reduce the heat and simmer for approximately 2 hours, stirring from time to time. If the sauce dries out too much, add a little more wine and be sure the heat is low. When the sauce is of a medium thickness, place everything into a deep baking dish and let it cool. Preheat the oven to 450°F.

Roll out enough pastry dough to cover a baking dish. Crimp the edges of crust around the baking dish and cut three vents in the top of the pastry to allow steam to escape. Bake at 450°F for 15 minutes, lower the heat to 350°F, and continue baking until the crust is golden brown.

SERVES 8.

# Birmingham Steak and Kidney Pie

2 pounds beef chuck roast, shoulder, or rump, cut into
1-inch cubes
1 pound lamb kidneys, cut into 1-inch cubes
2 tablespoons all-purpose flour
½ teaspoon salt
½ teaspoon pepper
2 cups beef bouillon
Pastry dough (your own or prepared mix)
1 egg, beaten

Season the flour with salt and pepper and dredge the beef
and kidney cubes thoroughly. In a pie pan or oven-proof
baking dish, place an egg cup or small funnel in center to
support the pastry dough cover of the pie. Put the floured
beef and kidney into the pan or dish around the egg cup or
funnel and pour in the bouillon until it comes three-quarters
up to the top of the meat. Don't bring the bouillon level with
the top of the meat or it will boil over in baking. Preheat the
oven to 450°F.

Roll out the pastry dough and cover the pie with it. Brush
the beaten egg over the top of the pastry and crimp the edges
around the dish. Cut small vents in the top of the pastry
crust.

Bake at 450°F for 25 minutes or until the pastry has risen.
Then lower the heat to 325°F and bake for approximately 1½
hours.

SERVES 6.

# Irish Stew

Many recipes for Irish stew are Americanized by additions of celery, carrots, etc. The real Irish stew had none of these, although cabbage was sometimes added.

    4 to 5 pounds beef chuck, top round, or flanken
            (boiling beef or short ribs)
    4 pounds potatoes, peeled
    1½ pounds onions
    1 tablespoon salt
    ½ teaspoon pepper
    2 cups (approximately) water
    1 pound red or green cabbage (optional), shredded

Cut one-third of the potatoes into flat slices and set aside. Slice ½ pound of the onions. Place the sliced onions across the bottom of a pot, then lay the potato slices over them. These will mix with the meat drippings and gravy during cooking and keep the stew from becoming too watery.

Cut the remainder of the potatoes in halves and place in the pot along with the meat. Cut the remaining onions in halves and add to stew. Season with salt and pepper and add enough water to just cover. Add the shredded cabbage, if desired, to the pot. Cook for 2 to 2½ hours over a low heat, stirring occasionally.

SERVES 4 TO 6.

*Serve with a dark ale or stout.*

# Highland Braised Beef

>       2 to 3 pounds beef chuck, top round, boneless
>               shoulder, or pot roast
>       2 tablespoons butter
>       ½ pound bacon, cut into 1-inch strips
>       4 carrots, sliced
>       2 onions, sliced
>       3 turnips, diced
>       ¼ teaspoon allspice
>       ¼ teaspoon marjoram
>       ½ teaspoon pepper
>       ¼ teaspoon parsley
>       ¼ teaspoon mace
>       2 cups beef bouillon

Preheat the oven to 325°F. In a large saucepan or skillet, melt the butter and add the bacon strips and vegetables. Sauté the vegetables until they are softened, then remove them from the pan. Sauté the meat in the same pan, browning evenly on all sides. Pour off the remainder of the butter in the pan and remove the meat.

In a large pot or oven-proof casserole, place the vegetables and bacon strips to form a bed. Mix all the spices and herbs together and sprinkle over the vegetables and bacon. Place the meat on top of the vegetables and add the bouillon. Cook, covered, for 2 to 2½ hours or until the meat is tender.

SERVES 4.

*Serve with vegetables in pot and a side dish of string beans.*

# Forfar Bridies

These little meatcakes were a favorite of J. M. Barrie, who is perhaps best known as the author of *Peter Pan*.

> 1½ pounds beef sirloin, shell steak, porterhouse, or top round
> ¼ teaspoon salt
> ¼ teaspoon pepper
> Pastry dough (your own or prepared mix)
> 1 cup beef suet, shredded or minced
> ½ cup onion, minced

Preheat the oven to 425°F. Flatten the steak with a mallet or rolling pin. Cut into strips 1 inch long and ½ inch wide. Sprinkle the strips with the salt and pepper and divide into 4 equal amounts.

Prepare the pastry dough and make 4 circles, each approximately ⅛ inch thick and at least 4 inches in diameter. Lay the meat strips over one-half of each circle of pastry dough, almost to the edge. Cover the steak strips with equal amounts of the suet and onion.

Fold over the other half of the pastry dough and crimp the edges together so the Bridies will have a half-moon shape. Make 2 little holes in the center of each. Bake until the pastry has risen, then lower the heat to 350°F and continue baking for approximately 45 minutes or until the pastry is golden.

SERVES 4.

*Mashed potatoes and a vegetable go well with Forfar Bridies.*

# Potted Hough

    1½ pounds beef shin, cut up
      2 pig's feet
      2 tablespoons butter
    ½ teaspoon salt
    ½ teaspoon pepper
      2 cloves
    ¼ teaspoon thyme
      2 bay leaves
    ¼ teaspoon rosemary
        Water

Wash the beef shin and pig's feet. Brown in the butter in a skillet, remove from the pan, and let drain. Place into a pot with the herbs and spices, cover with cold water, and simmer slowly for approximately 2½ hours or until the meat falls from the bones.

Remove the meat and bones, reserving the stock. Remove the bay leaves and discard. Cut the meat into thick, irregular strips. Put the meat into a bowl or mold. Return the stock to the pot and cook to reduce to approximately 2 to 2½ cups. Pour over the meat in the bowl or mold without straining. (Retention of the gelatine in the liquid is important.) Allow the finished dish to set. To serve, remove the potted hough from the bowl or mold.

SERVES 4.

*May be sliced or cut into narrow strips and placed over a bed of lettuce and tomato; can be served chilled or warmed.*

# Manchester Oxtail Stew

This dish is cooked by slowly stewing it. Many prefer to serve it, reheated, the day after it is made.

4 to 5 pounds oxtails (2 tails, about 2 to 2½ pounds
        each), cut into serving-size pieces
1¼ cups white beans (often called navy or pea beans)
½ teaspoon salt
¼ teaspoon pepper
1 cup all-purpose flour
3 tablespoons lard, fat, or vegetable shortening
2 medium-sized onions, chopped
2 leeks, sliced
4 carrots, sliced
1 cup beef bouillon
2 cups red wine (preferably Burgundy)
½ teaspoon dry mustard
3 bay leaves
½ teaspoon thyme

If dried beans are used, they should be soaked in cold water overnight. Blend the salt and pepper into the flour. Dredge the oxtail pieces thoroughly until each is well coated. Put them into a huge pot with the lard (or other fat) and sauté until browned and golden. Add the onions, leeks, carrots, and beans and continue cooking for 10 minutes over a medium heat. Add the bouillon, stir, and cook another 5 minutes. Add enough of the wine to cover the ingredients, bring to a boil, and stir thoroughly. Add the mustard and bay leaves and stir again. Reduce the heat and cover. Cook over low heat for 1 hour, then remove the bay leaves and sprinkle in the thyme. Cook for 1 hour longer. At the end of the second hour, stir thoroughly and add more wine if needed. Simmer, covered, for 45 more minutes.

Before serving, skim the fat off the top. If the fat is difficult to remove, chill the pot in the refrigerator until the fat hardens enough to remove easily. Reheat and serve. If serving the following day, remove the fat just before reheating.
SERVES 4 TO 6.

# Shooter's Pie

August 12 marks the beginning of the shooting season in England. Parliament adjourns before this date, and for weeks ahead of time the gamekeepers of every estate and tract of land send bulletins on the condition of the birds.

The following dish can be made ready and put on to cook when the shooters return from the field.

    4 rib or loin lamb chops
    2 pounds mashed potatoes
    1 teaspoon salt
    1/4 teaspoon pepper
    7 tablespoons butter
    1 cup beef bouillon
    1/2 teaspoon Worcestershire sauce

Preheat the oven to 350°F. Prepare the mashed potatoes. Beat in the salt, pepper, and 4 tablespoons of the butter. Use 1 tablespoon of the butter to thoroughly grease an oven-proof casserole dish. Line the bottom and sides of the dish with roughly half of the mashed potatoes and set aside.

When ready to cook, sauté the lamb chops in the remaining 2 tablespoons of butter in a skillet. Brown on both sides, approximately 5 minutes per side. Remove and keep warm. Add the beef bouillon, bring to a boil, and then simmer over a very low heat.

Place the lamb chops in the potato-lined dish, reserving the bouillon gravy. Pour the Worcestershire sauce over the chops and cover with the rest of the potatoes to form a pielike crust. Bake for 1/2 hour. Pour the bouillon gravy on top and serve.

SERVES 2 TO 4.

# Lamb Breast with Rice and Egg Stuffing

Dr. Kitchiner, author of early English cookbooks, had a strict rule for his small, private dinner parties, which he posted on a placard: "Come at Seven—Go Before Eleven." At his formal dinners, he decreed that "to insure the punctual attendance of those gastrophilists . . . invited to join this high tribunal of taste," no guest be admitted "of whatever eminence his appetite, after the hour at which [it had been announced] the specimens are ready."

1 large breast of lamb (2 to 3½ pounds)
2 onions, chopped
1 red sweet pepper, diced
2 tablespoons butter
1 cup long-grained rice
1 cup celery, chopped
¼ teaspoon salt
¼ teaspoon pepper
1 cup beef bouillon
1 cup raisins
4 hard-boiled eggs, thinly sliced

Preheat the oven to 350°F. Have the butcher trim and prepare the lamb roast for rolling, flattening it slightly. Lay the lamb breast on a flat surface.

Sauté the onions and sweet pepper in the butter in a large skillet. Add the rice, celery, salt, and pepper and pour in the beef bouillon. Simmer for 15 minutes and add the raisins. Stir, mix thoroughly, and remove from the heat.

Spread the stuffing over the lamb breast. Place the thin slices of hard-boiled eggs over the stuffing and carefully roll the lamb lengthwise from the ends. When finished, fasten with skewers or toothpicks.

Cook in an open roasting pan for 25 minutes per pound plus an additional 20 minutes. Slice the finished breast so that each slice of meat contains a slice of egg.

SERVES 4.

*A good rosé or one of the sparkling wines goes well here.*

# Roast Saddle of Lamb

Dr. William Kitchiner's 1822 cookbook, *The Cook's Oracle*, was a philosophical as well as practical volume for those who tend the kitchen. At one point he listed "seven chances against even the most simple dish being presented to the mouth in absolute perfection; for instance, a leg of mutton. First—the mutton must be good; 2nd—it must have been kept a good time; 3rd—must be roasted at a good fire; 4th—by a good cook; 5th—who must be in good temper; 6th—with all this felicitous combination you must have good luck, and 7th—Good Appetite. The meat and the mouths which are to eat it must be ready for each other, at the same moment."

    1 saddle of lamb (5 to 7 pounds)
    ½ teaspoon salt
    ½ teaspoon pepper
    1½ teaspoons almonds, shelled and then powdered
    1 cup peach nectar
    12 mint leaves or 3 tablespoons mint jelly

Have the butcher score the fat on the lamb in a crisscross pattern. Bring the lamb to room temperature. Mix the salt, pepper, and powdered almonds. (If the powdered variety is not available, the almonds may be powdered by using a mortar and pestle or by hammering inside a cloth.) Rub the mixture generously into the lamb fat. Preheat the oven to 325°F.

Line the bottom of a roasting pan with the peach nectar and mint leaves. (If mint leaves are unavailable, spread the mint jelly and ¼ cup of water on the bottom of the roasting pan. Heat slowly until the mint jelly liquefies. Then add the peach nectar.)

Place a rack in the pan and put the lamb on it. Roast, 15 minutes for rare meat, 30 for medium, basting with peach nectar every 15 minutes. Increase the heat to 350°F and continue cooking for another 30 minutes, basting with peach nectar every 15 minutes. If the nectar in the pan dries out, add more.

Turn off the heat and let the lamb stay in the oven for 5 to 7 minutes more. Baste once again before serving.

SERVES 6.

# Spring Lamb Hot Pot

 2 pounds spring lamb, half from the shoulder and half
   from the neck, cut into 1½-inch cubes
 3 medium-sized onions, quartered
 6 medium-sized carrots, cut into quarters
 3 cups beef stock or bouillon
 ½ teaspoon salt
 ¼ teaspoon pepper
 4 tomatoes, quartered
 2 cups fresh or frozen peas
 6 Herb Dumplings (optional)

*Herb Dumplings*

 1½ cups all-purpose flour
   2 teaspoons baking powder
 ½ teaspoon salt
 ½ cup beef suet, finely chopped
   Water
 ¼ teaspoon sage
 ¼ teaspoon rosemary
 ¼ teaspoon chives
 ¼ teaspoon parsley
 ¼ teaspoon basil

Preheat the oven to 325°F.

Place the lamb cubes in a pot or oven-proof casserole, along with the onions and carrots. Add the stock or bouillon, salt, and pepper. Cook, tightly covered, for 1½ hours. Add the tomatoes and peas. If the stock is cooked away, add a little more. Then add the Herb Dumplings, if desired. Stir and continue cooking, uncovered, for an additional 30 minutes.

To prepare the Herb Dumplings, sift the flour, baking powder, and salt together. Add the suet and mix thoroughly, using a wooden spoon to blend the mixture. Carefully add just enough water to make the mixture firm enough to allow handling without falling apart. Add all the herbs and mix again. Add more water if needed.

Lightly flour your hands and roll the mixture into dumplings, as you would make meatballs. When adding the dumplings to the pot, make sure that the stock is bubbling and that there's enough to coat the dumplings.

SERVES 4 TO 6.

# Shepherd's Pie

        1 pound lamb, ground once
        1 large onion, finely chopped
        2 teaspoons lard
        ¼ teaspoon pepper
        ½ teaspoon sage
        ½ teaspoon thyme
        ¼ teaspoon rosemary
        ½ teaspoon salt
     1½ cups beef bouillon
        1 large carrot, sliced or cut into small pieces
        1 can (10 ounces) green peas, frozen or cooked
        1 pound mashed potatoes
        3 tablespoons butter

Preheat the oven to 400°F. Sauté the onion in the lard until it is softened. Add the ground lamb and brown for 5 minutes over a low heat. Add the spices, herbs, and salt, stir thoroughly, and then add the bouillon. Place the mixture into an oven-proof dish or pie pan. Add a layer of the carrots and the peas and cover with the mashed potatoes. Put small pieces of butter on top. Bake for approximately 30 to 45 minutes or until the top of potatoes is browned and crisp.

SERVES 4.

# Champagned Ham

Ham (in some form) and champagne are traditional for ushering in the New Year. January was once called *Wolfmonat* (wolf-month) by the ancient Saxons, which meant the month when wolves were hungriest and attacked the most people. Later, they called it *After-yule*. New Year's Day is not as old as is generally believed. January 1 did not become the first day of the new year until 1752 in England; 1600 in Scotland; 1564 in France; 1700 in Germany, Holland, and Russia; and 1753 in Sweden.

            14 to 18 pound ham, precooked
                1 bottle pink champagne
                4 tablespoons orange juice
                2 tablespoons pineapple juice
                2 tablespoons honey
                6 tablespoons dark brown sugar
               24 whole cloves
                1 large can pineapple rings
                3 tablespoons peach brandy

Have the butcher score the fat on top of the ham in a crisscross, diamond pattern. Pour the champagne in a large pot, place the ham in the champagne, and marinate overnight in the refrigerator.

On the following day, remove the ham from the pot, reserving the champagne, and bring to room temperature. Let stand for 30 minutes.

Mix the orange juice, pineapple juice, honey, and brown sugar together. Rub the mixture generously all over the ham. Place 1 clove in the center of each diamond on top of the ham. Put the ham on a rack in a roasting pan and pour 1½ cups of the reserved champagne into the bottom of the pan.

Place in the oven and bring the heat to 325°F. Bake for 1 hour. Pour another cup of the champagne over the ham and add more to bottom of pan if the amount of liquid has been substantially reduced. Bake 15 minutes longer and baste with pan drippings and champagne. Bake for 30 minutes more. Place the pineapple rings over the ham and baste again with pan drippings and champagne. Bake for an additional 30 minutes.

When ready to serve, heat the brandy, spoon over the ham, and then ignite.

SERVES 12 TO 14.

*This dish is delicious served cold the next day.*

# Toad-in-the-Hole

> 1 pound sausages (any variety, though pork sausages
> are often preferred)
> 1 cup pancake batter
> 1 tablespoon lard
> 3 tomatoes, cut into quarters
> ¼ pound mushrooms, sliced
> ¼ teaspoon nutmeg
> ¼ teaspoon pepper

Prepare the pancake batter. Fry the sausages in a skillet. Preheat the oven to 450°F.

In a 10- to 12-inch-square baking dish or pie plate, melt the lard over a low heat, rubbing or brushing some along the sides of the plate. Put the fried sausages into the baking dish or pie plate, along with the tomatoes and mushrooms. Add the nutmeg and pepper and stir. Pour the pancake batter over everything and bake at 450°F for 10 to 12 minutes, until the batter begins to rise.

Lower the heat to 350°F and bake until the batter is golden brown, approximately 20 to 30 minutes.

SERVES 4 TO 6.

*A hearty beer makes a satisfying companion.*

# Casserole of Grouse

    2 grouse, cleaned and ready to cook (quail, partridge,
        or squab may be substituted)
    2 tablespoons flour
    6 slices bacon
    ½ cup lard
    1 large or 2 small turnips, diced
    1½ onions, chopped
    3 carrots, thinly sliced
    2 cups chicken broth or game stock
    ½ teaspoon salt
    ½ teaspoon pepper
    2 bay leaves
    3 tomatoes, cut into halves

Preheat the oven to 300°F. Put the grouse on a flat surface
and flour lightly on all sides. Cut the bacon into strips ½
inch wide. Fry the grouse in ¼ cup of the lard in a skillet for
15 minutes, adding the bacon strips halfway through. When
finished, remove the grouse and bacon to a casserole or earthenware pot.

Add the remainder of the fat and sauté the turnips, onion,
and carrots. Add the chicken broth or game stock slowly,
bring to a boil, and cook until the broth thickens. Add the
salt and pepper, stir, and pour the mixture over the grouse.
Add the bay leaves and tomatoes. Cover and cook for 2 hours
or until the grouse are tender. Remove the bay leaves and
serve.

SERVES 4.

# Stuffed Roast Goose with Chestnuts

Holiday prices for meat are not only the custom of modern suppliers. In 1290, under Edward I, the Common Council of London fixed the price of "a fat lamb" at "sixpence from Christmas to Shrovetide, the rest of the year, fourpence." They did the same with all meats at holidays.

> 1 goose (10 to 12 pounds), prepared for roasting
> 2 large onions, chopped
> ¼ stick butter
> ½ teaspoon salt
> ¼ teaspoon pepper
> 2 cups bread crumbs
> 2 tablespoons sage
> 1 cup chicken bouillon
> 2 pounds chestnuts, shelled and skinned

Wash and dry the goose and bring to room temperature. Preheat the oven to 350°F. To make the stuffing, sauté the onions in the butter in a skillet until golden. Reduce the heat and add the salt, pepper, bread crumbs, and sage. Mix thoroughly and add half the bouillon to moisten. Remove from the heat and mix. If not moist enough, add the remaining ½ cup of bouillon and mix again.

When the stuffing is cool enough to handle, stuff the goose, not too tightly, and close the opening with a toothpick or skewer. Place the goose on a rack in a roasting pan. Bake for 1 hour, then drain off excess fat. Continue roasting for 2½ hours. At that time, drain the fat out of the roasting pan (a little will remain). Add the chestnuts to the pan, return to the oven, and roast for an additional 45 minutes. (Total roasting time should be approximately 4 to 4½ hours.)

SERVES 8.

*String beans and a good Burgundy go well here.*

# Pot Roast Rabbit

    2 rabbits, cleaned, skinned, and cut into serving-size
       pieces (eliminate the head, giblets, and other
       interior parts)
    1 quart water
    1 cup vinegar
    ½ pound bacon, thickly cut
    2 tablespoons flour
    2 teaspoons salt
    ½ teaspoon pepper
    1 cup chicken bouillon or broth
    1 teaspoon dry mustard
    ¾ pint milk

Soak the cut-up rabbits in water and vinegar for 2 to 4 hours. Dry each piece and set aside on a dry towel or in a dish. Fry the bacon, drain off the fat, and set aside.

Mix the flour with the salt and pepper and dredge the pieces of rabbit. Sauté the meat in oil in a skillet until evenly browned on all sides. Remove from the skillet and put into a pot or flame-proof casserole dish. Place pieces of drained bacon over the rabbit.

Simmer in bouillon or broth over a low heat for approximately 1 hour, turning the pieces occasionally for even cooking. Mix the dry mustard into the milk, add the mixture to the pot, stir, and cook for an additional 30 minutes. Pour the gravy in the pot over the rabbit when serving.

Serves 4.

*A good Riesling adds a nice touch to this different kind of pot roast.*

# Kingdom of Fife Pie

2 rabbits, cleaned, skinned, and cut into serving-size
　　pieces (reserve the heads)
2 tablespoons lard
4 medium-sized hard-boiled eggs, cut into quarters
½ pound pickled (cured) pork, diced or shredded
½ teaspoon salt
¼ teaspoon pepper
½ teaspoon nutmeg
3 cups chicken bouillon or rabbit stock
　　Pastry dough (your own or prepared mix)
1 egg, beaten

Sauté the rabbit pieces in the lard in a skillet to brown
evenly on all sides. Drain and remove to a pie plate or casserole, placing them in the center. Arrange the hard-boiled
egg quarters around the sides of the dish. Preheat the oven
to 425°F.

Place the pickled pork on top of the rabbit. Mix the salt,
pepper, and nutmeg and sprinkle over everything. Pour in
the chicken bouillon (enough to fill two-thirds of the dish).
(If time permits, make a stock from the rabbit heads, fore-
legs, and giblets.) Cover with pastry dough, crimping the
edges, and glaze by brushing on the beaten egg. Cut vents
in the pastry crust.

Bake at 425°F for 30 minutes, then reduce the heat to 300°F
and cook for 2 hours.

SERVES 6.

# ∼4∼
# FRANCE

FRENCH cuisine departed from all other cuisines in one major respect. The great dishes that are synonymous with French cooking today did not grow out of the geography, the climate, and the social conditions as was the case in other lands. For the first time in culinary history, a style and manner of cooking was the result of a series of individual creators; inventors with pots and pans as their tools; and artists who painted with beef and pork, veal and poultry—the *grand chefs*. French haute cuisine has been part of the world's culinary riches ever since.

But even creators require the proper atmosphere, and this was supplied by the times and the personalities. When French cuisine began to emerge from Italian influence during post-Renaissance years, the first of the Bourbon kings took the throne of France, followed by Louis XIII, Louis XIV, Louis XV, and Louis XVI. All of these monarchs delighted in grand dining. They may have had only self-indulgence and royal rivalries in mind, but they supplied support, enthusiasm, and official expectations to their chefs. Their life-styles demanded voluminous entertaining and sensational culinary efforts. Louis XIV gave affairs requiring hundreds of people to prepare and serve, banquets which made those of the ancient pharaohs and Roman emperors look like school lunches. When he was but eighteen years of age, he presided at a banquet where 168 different dishes were served. During everyday dining at the palace, a company of royal guards would march through the various rooms leading a procession of other court dignitaries and crying out: "The King's meat. Stand aside, the King's meat."

In this royal atmosphere the great chefs were urged to invent new dishes, a culinary climate that lasted far longer, and was far more pervasive, than the Bourbon monarchies themselves. This climate produced the great French chefs with their international following—the Vatels, La Varennes, Carêmes, Marins, Mornays, and Escoffiers. The French haute cuisine is largely the result of these great chefs and their personal creations, as are the rich, thick, and heavy sauces

113

the world has since associated with French cooking. Unlike in other lands, the sauces were not concocted to make tough meat more palatable. The chefs, under constant pressure from their royal masters, realized that there were only so many ways they could serve meat and that only a limited number of cuts and styles were to be had. Something more had to be added, and their answer was the sauces that would allow an infinite variety of flavors to invest the meat and the accompanying dishes.

The world in general still thinks of French cooking in terms of its rich sauces. But the haute cuisine and its sauces was, and for the most part still is, the sphere of the professional chef. The main body of French cuisine is found in what we call French provincial cooking—an unfortunate term because it connotes, especially to Americans, something backwoods, inferior, of less sophistication. In some countries this interpretation of provincial may well hold true, including our own, but it is a grievous misapplication to French cooking. The cooking of the provinces might be a more accurate term for the dishes of the various regions of France prepared with their own special, regional touches—the cooking of Brittany, the Loire, the Savoie, Alsace-Lorraine, Provence, the Perigord, and Gascogny. In these and the other provinces is to be found the main body of French cooking. This cooking is different from the haute cuisine, not less.

But whether the grand chefs or the Burgundy housewife stirred the kettle, the land played a role in the tastiness of the final result. In France there was no problem with the land being too arid to support more than the hardy sheep and goat, or with a climate too fierce for most game birds. This land offered every kind of meat and fowl and every kind of vegetable within its borders. The distance between field and table has never been very great in France, adding the advantage of freshness and helping to achieve the subtleties of blend and balance that have become one of the hallmarks of French cooking.

But another major factor existed in France that was missing in other countries and was perhaps most responsible for the place French cuisine has achieved. In almost all countries ruled by monarchies or a powerful ruling class, there existed the aristocracy and the peasants, the rulers and the serfs and nothing in between. High eating, fancy dishes, and the pleasures of the banquet tables would never touch the poor. In France, however, there developed what could be called a middle class and a peasantry equally interested in good eating—tradesmen, small landowners, craftsmen, independent farmers. Indeed, before the French Revolution, Voltaire attacked his followers for their avid interest in eating and the pleasures of the table, which he regarded as paralleling aristocratic self-indulgence. Despite Voltaire's admonitions, the loving attention to food well prepared and well served became a part of every level of French society, a heritage carried to this very day.

Not only did the grand chefs create a repertoire of dishes, and the provinces contribute their regional culinary wisdom and traditional specialties, but the manner of dining as we know it today can be credited to France. A chef to Louis XIV, François Pierre de La Varenne, brought a new approach to the serving of dinner. Displeased with the then-popular way of serving everything at once, with every variety of meat conflicting with each other and with the rest of the dishes, he set down guidelines for the orderly serving of courses. He turned gargantuan eating into dining. Planned menus, served in a specific order, finally took hold with all the great chefs and, in time, with all manner of dining. The menu, from the Latin word *minutus*, was not used until 1541 and then as a general guide only to the host. And the first restaurant to be truly that—a place to dine away from home, to select one's own menu from many offered—was established in Paris in 1782 by Chef Beauvilliers, once steward to Louis XVIII. It is to the everlasting credit of Beauvilliers that he realized that the great dishes of French cuisine were meant to be shared by many.

But to cook as the French cook is not simply to purchase the proper cuts of meat and the correct vegetables, and to follow a recipe. It is not only sauces and subtleties, delicacy, and blends. It is to add an extra measure of something not in recipes or ingredients. It is to enjoy cooking and to approach the very act of cooking with love. It is to take pleasure in the touch, sight, and smell of going to market, to enjoy and to savor every step that goes into making the finished dish. This culinary tender loving care was basic to the creations of the great chefs and the everyday meals of the simplest of French households. The results will be there on your *bonne table*.

# Roast Boneless Top Loin
*(Contrefilet Roti)*

      1 boneless top loin of beef (about 5 pounds), rolled
         and tied and trimmed of excess fat
      ½ teaspoon salt
      ¼ teaspoon pepper
      4 tablespoons salad oil
      6 medium-sized potatoes, cut into halves
      1 stick butter
      1 tablespoon tarragon

Preheat the oven to 450°F. Season the boneless top loin with the salt and pepper, and brush on the oil, including the ends. Put the meat on a rack in a baking dish large enough to accommodate the potatoes. Cook for 15 minutes, then put the potato halves into the baking pan and reduce the heat to 350°F.

Continue cooking 1 hour for rare, 1¼ hours for medium, or 1½ hours for well done, basting occasionally with natural juices in the pan. Serve the potatoes with the meat, using juices from the pan as a sauce.

A simple additional sauce may be made by melting the stick of butter in a saucepan and adding the tarragon. Serve this sauce on the side with a spoon or brush.

SERVES 10.

*Accompany with a very cold sparkling red Burgundy.*

# Steak Vin Rouge

On Shrove Tuesday—the day before Ash Wednesday, which begins Lent—the butchers of Paris celebrated *Boeuf Gras* (fat ox) day. A fat ox was paraded through the streets as a reminder for the day when, after Lent, it would be time to eat meat again. Rival butchers competed to supply the ox that was the fattest and sleekest and in the best condition. *Boeuf Gras* day became a carnival festivity with all sorts of marchers eventually taking part.

    1 sirloin or porterhouse steak, cut 1½ to 2 inches thick
    11 tablespoons butter
    ½ cup scallions, chopped
    1 bay leaf
    ¼ teaspoon basil
    ¼ teaspoon rosemary
    2 cups dry red wine
    1 cup beef bouillon
    1 tablespoon flour
    1 teaspoon lemon juice
    1 tablespoon salad oil
    ½ teaspoon salt
    ¼ teaspoon pepper

In a saucepan, melt 2 tablespoons of the butter. Add the scallions and sauté until they turn soft and gold. Add the bay leaf, basil, rosemary, and red wine. Stir and simmer over a medium heat for approximately 10 minutes or until the wine is reduced by half.

Strain the wine mixture through a fine sieve into a bowl and discard the herbs and scallions. Return the strained wine to the saucepan and add the bouillon. Bring to a boil for 1 minute, then set aside.

Soften 8 tablespoons of the butter until it is easy to beat. Add the flour and lemon juice and mix thoroughly. Set aside.

In a skillet, melt the oil and the remaining tablespoon of

butter together. Season the steak with salt and pepper, place in the skillet, and sear over a high heat, 3 minutes on each side. Reduce to a moderate heat and sauté for 5 to 7 minutes on each side for rare or 10 minutes on each side for medium. Remove the steak and keep warm in a heated oven.

Pour the wine-bouillon into the skillet and bring to a boil over a moderate heat. Reduce to a very low heat and blend in the creamed butter mixture a little at a time, until the wine and butter are thoroughly blended. Pour over the steak and serve the remainder of the sauce separately.

SERVES 3 TO 4.

# Entrecote Brittany

> 4 entrecotes (eye of shell, each 1 to 1¼ inches thick),
>     boneless, fat and muscle removed
> 4 tablespoons salad oil
> 1 tablespoon salt
> 1 teaspoon pepper
> 1 stick butter
> 2 shallots, very finely chopped
> 1 tablespoon parsley, chopped
> 1½ teaspoons lemon juice

Rub each entrecote with oil, season with salt and pepper, and set aside. Soften the butter almost to melting. Add the chopped shallots, parsley, and lemon juice. Mix until smoothly blended together.

Put the entrecotes on a grill or broiler. Sear 5 minutes on each side for rare or 7 minutes on each side for medium-rare. Remove the entrecotes from the heat, spread the butter mixture over the top side of each one, and then put in a saucepan and cook over a low heat for another 2 minutes.

SERVES 4.

*Serve with a border of peas around each entrecote. A dry Pommard goes well with this dish.*

# Veal Escallops in Cream

8 veal escallops
¾ tablespoon salt
1 teaspoon pepper
4 teaspoons lemon juice
2 hard-boiled eggs
8 thin slices ham
4 tablespoons butter
½ cup white wine
1 cup heavy cream

Season the veal escallops with the salt and pepper and sprinkle lemon juice on each. Slice the hard-boiled eggs into 8 thin slices. Lay 1 slice of ham and 1 slice of egg on each escallop. Roll up each piece and fasten with a toothpick or tie with thread.

Cook the escallops in butter for 5 minutes. Pour in the white wine and then the cream. Stir the mixture and simmer the escallops for another 2 minutes, turning them frequently to coat with the sauce. Cover and simmer for 3 more minutes.

SERVES 4 TO 6.

*A Chardonnay goes perfectly with this dish.*

# Veal with Tomatoes

*(Veau aux Tomates)*

>     1 boneless veal rump roast (5 to 6 pounds)
>     2 cloves garlic, coarsely diced
>     ½ teaspoon salt
>     ¼ teaspoon pepper
>     3 tablespoons salad oil
>     9 tomatoes (whole)
>    16 small white onions (whole), peeled
>     ½ teaspoon rosemary
>     ¼ teaspoon thyme
>     1 cup chicken bouillon

Have the butcher roll and bone the rump of veal. Using the tip of a sharp knife, press each piece of the coarsely diced garlic into the veal on the top and on both sides. Distribute evenly across meat. Season with the salt and pepper.

In a large kettle, heat the oil, put in the rolled veal, and brown on all sides over a moderate heat. When browned, reduce the heat and add the onions, tomatoes, rosemary, and thyme. Simmer over a low heat for 30 minutes. Pour in the bouillon and continue cooking for at least another 1 hour or until the veal is tender. Serve with the onions and tomatoes around the veal roast.

SERVES 4 TO 6.

*A dry Bordeaux accompanies this dish well.*

# Sautéed Veal Kidneys
*(Rognons Sautés)*

4 whole veal kidneys
4 tablespoons butter
1 dozen shallots, chopped
1 cup Madeira wine
½ pound mushrooms, sliced
¼ teaspoon salt
⅛ teaspoon pepper

Have the butcher trim off all fat from the kidneys. Melt the butter in a flame-proof dish over a low heat. Sauté the kidneys, whole, for about 15 minutes in the butter, turning frequently until they are lightly browned. Then remove the kidneys, set aside, and cover to keep warm.

Add chopped shallots to the butter in the dish, stir, and sauté for 2 minutes. Then add the wine and stir. Raise the heat and boil the wine until it reduces and thickens, approximately 5 minutes. Add the mushrooms, salt, and pepper, stirring vigorously for 1 minute. Then let the sauce simmer for 4 minutes longer.

Slice the kidneys into fairly thin slices, return them to the dish, and stir until coated with the sauce and heated through.

SERVES 3 TO 4.

*Serve with potato pancakes.*

# Saddle of Lamb Roast
*(Selle d'Agneau)*

> 1 saddle of lamb (6 to 8 pounds)
> ½ teaspoon salt
> ½ teaspoon freshly ground pepper
> 2 teaspoons ginger
> 1 teaspoon paprika
> ½ onion, grated
> 1 teaspoon lemon juice
> ½ cup olive oil
> 1 cup beef bouillon
> 2 tablespoons cognac

Have excess fat trimmed from the lamb. Mix all the other ingredients except the beef bouillon and cognac into the olive oil to form a thin paste. Spread the paste over the lamb and let stand at room temperature for at least 2 hours. When ready to cook, preheat the oven to 350°F, place the lamb on a rack in a roasting pan, and roast for 1¼ hours for rare or 1½ hours for medium. Baste frequently.

For the sauce, remove the lamb from the pan, skim off the surface fat, and pour the rest of the juices into a saucepan. Add the beef bouillon and cognac, heat, stir well, and serve in a separate sauceboat.

SERVES 6 TO 8.

*Serve with a purée of potatoes in which cooked peas have been mixed, and a chilled Chablis.*

# Kidneys in Madeira
*(Rognons Madeira)*

12 lamb kidneys
4 tablespoons butter
¼ cup parsley, chopped
1 medium-sized onion, finely chopped
¼ teaspoon chives, chopped
¼ teaspoon salt
⅛ teaspoon freshly ground pepper
6 mushrooms, thinly sliced
1 tablespoon flour
½ cup Madeira wine

Have the butcher clean kidneys of all covering membranes and remove all fat. The kidneys should then be thinly sliced. Melt the butter in a large skillet and add the parsley, onion, and chives. Sauté for 3 minutes, stirring constantly. Season with salt and pepper. Add the sliced mushrooms and the kidneys and continue to cook over a moderate heat, stirring constantly, until almost done.

Sprinkle in the flour and add the Madeira. Stir the mixture well and cook for another 2 to 3 minutes.

SERVES 4.

*Serve on slices of bread fried in butter.*

# Pork and Prunes
*(Noisettes de Porc aux Pruneaux)*

*Noisettes* is the French term for hazelnuts. These little hazelnuts of pork are usually served with a cream sauce. For these diet-conscious days, we also offer a less rich version.

>         8 *noisettes* of pork cut from the loin (approximately
>             1½ inches thick), trimmed, boned, and tied
>     1½ pounds (36) dried prunes
>     1½ cups dry white wine
>     ½ teaspoon salt
>     ¼ teaspoon freshly ground pepper
>     ½ cup flour
>       1 tablespoon oil
>       2 tablespoons butter

*Cream Sauce*

>     ½ to ¾ cup heavy cream
>         1½ tablespoons red currant jelly
>           1 tablespoon lemon juice

*Mild Sauce*

>       ½ cup red currant jelly
>       2 tablespoons sherry

Have the butcher prepare the *noisettes* of pork. Soak the prunes in the white wine for at least 4 hours, overnight if possible. Then cook them over a low heat in the wine for 10 minutes. Remove and reserve the wine and prunes separately.

Coat the *noisettes* with the salt and pepper, then dust lightly with the flour. In a heavy skillet, melt the oil and butter together over a low heat, put in the *noisettes*, and brown on both sides, approximately 5 minutes. Remove the *noisettes*, pour the fat from the skillet, and then add the wine used to soak the prunes. Return the pork to the skillet, cover, and cook gently for 30 minutes or until the meat is tender.

To prepare the Cream Sauce, in a separate pan, pour in the red currant jelly, lemon juice, and heavy cream. Boil over a moderate heat, stirring constantly, until the sauce thickens. Add the prunes and continue stirring until the sauce has thickened enough to cling to the back of the spoon. Place the *noisettes* on a serving plate, lift the prunes from the sauce with a slotted spoon, and arrange around the *noisettes*. Pour the remainder of the sauce over everything.

For the Mild Sauce, heat the red currant jelly over a low heat, stirring constantly, in a separate pan. When the jelly is heated through and reduced to a liquid, add the prunes and continue cooking until the prunes are heated. Then add the sherry and cook for 2 minutes longer. To serve, follow the directions given for the Cream Sauce.

SERVES 4.

# Pork Chops, Potatoes, and Ham
*(Terrine de Porc au Pomme de Terre et Cham)*

4 loin or rib pork chops, 1 to 1¼ inches thick
2 cloves garlic, cut into quarters
8 juniper berries
2 pounds potatoes, peeled and thinly sliced
2 medium-sized onions, sliced
2 tablespoons butter
¼ pound sliced ham
½ teaspoon salt
¼ teaspoon pepper
1½ cups white wine

Preheat the oven to 350°F. Into each pork chop press 2 of the quarter-cloves of garlic, 1 piece near the bone and the other in the center. Then press in 2 of the juniper berries near the garlic pieces in each chop. Layer half of the potato and onion slices into an oven-proof terrine or pot.

Brown the pork chops on both sides in the butter, then place them on top of the potatoes and onions in the pot. Cover with the remaining potato and onion slices and the ham, season everything with salt and pepper, and pour the wine into the pot. Cover and cook for 45 minutes to 1 hour. Spoon off whatever fat has risen to the top.

SERVES 2.

*Serve out of the pot or terrine with a well-chilled rosé.*

# Chicken Flamed with Cognac and Sautéed in Cream Sauce

    1 frying or roasting chicken (3 to 4 pounds)
    6 tablespoons butter
    2 tablespoons salad oil
    2 onions, diced
    1 clove garlic, diced
    ½ cup mushrooms, chopped
    1 cup chicken stock or bouillon
    ½ teaspoon salt
    ½ teaspoon white pepper
    ½ cup cognac
    ¾ cup heavy cream
    ½ cup white wine

Brown the chicken in 4 tablespoons of the butter and the oil in a large skillet. Turn frequently over a low heat.

While the chicken is browning, cook the onions, garlic, and mushrooms in the remaining 2 tablespoons of butter for 5 minutes in a separate pan, stirring often. Add the chicken stock or bouillon, cook over a high heat for another 3 minutes, reduce the heat, and simmer for 1¼ hours.

Pour fat from the skillet containing the chicken, then season the pieces with salt and pepper. Pour the cognac carefully over all the pieces and ignite. As it flames, move the skillet carefully back and forth until the flame dies out.

Stir the vegetables and stock and cook over a moderate heat for 3 minutes. Then pour over the chicken pieces and cook over a moderate heat for 45 minutes or until the chicken is tender. Add more stock, if necessary, and baste the chicken pieces during cooking.

When the chicken pieces are done, remove them from the skillet and keep warm in a hot oven. Pour the heavy cream into the skillet with the stock and vegetable mixture and cook over a high heat, stirring vigorously. Add the wine, continue cooking for 3 minutes, but do not boil. Pour the sauce over the chicken pieces.

SERVES 4.

*Garnish with sprigs of parsley.*

# Chicken Cocotte

       1 chicken (3 to 4 pounds), cut into serving-size pieces
       ½ teaspoon salt
       ½ teaspoon freshly ground pepper
       2 tablespoons butter
       2 tablespoons salad oil
       ½ pound fat bacon, cubed
       5 scallions, chopped
       3 medium-sized carrots, cut into 1-inch-long sections
       ¼ teaspoon thyme
       ¼ teaspoon marjoram
       ¼ teaspoon rosemary
       2 cups red wine
         Chicken bouillon (if needed)

Season the cut-up chicken pieces with the salt and pepper.
In a heavy *cocotte*, terrine, or casserole, heat the butter and
oil together. Put in the cubed bacon and sauté over a moderate heat until the bacon pieces begin to turn golden. Remove with a slotted spoon. Add the scallions and carrots and
cook over a moderate heat, stirring frequently, until the vegetables begin to soften. Add the chicken pieces and brown on
all sides.

When the chicken pieces are browned, return the bacon
pieces to the *cocotte*. Add the thyme, marjoram, and rosemary and stir. Then pour in the wine. Cover the *cocotte* and
simmer until the chicken is tender, approximately 45 minutes to an hour. If the wine sauce reduces too quickly, add a
little chicken bouillon.

SERVES 3 TO 4.

*A cold Graves accompanies this dish well.*

# Casserole Canard

St. Hubert's day marks the beginning of the hunting season in France. The hunting dogs are brought to the local church, low mass is said, a piper blows a fanfare, and all the dogs are let loose to race to the priest for a personal pat, a piece of blessed bread, and a friendly word before going off to the hunt.

> 1 duck (5 to 6 pounds), cut into parts
> 5 tablespoons butter
> 2 tablespoons salad oil
> ½ cup bacon, diced
> 1 dozen small white onions
> ¼ cup flour
> 2 cups chicken bouillon
> 1 stalk celery, diced
> ½ teaspoon fresh fennel (or seeds)
> 1 teaspoon paprika
> 1½ teaspoons sugar
> 6 slices bread
> 3 cups red currant jelly

A large oven-proof casserole is required for this dish. The duck should fit into the casserole with breathing room around it.

Melt 2 tablespoons of the butter and the oil in the casserole. Sauté the bacon and the onions for 7 minutes or until the onions start to turn golden.

Add the duck to the casserole, brown on all sides, turning to do so, and finish with the breast side up. When the duck is browned, dust with flour, remove from the casserole, and add all the other ingredients except the bread and jelly. Stir and return the duck to the casserole. Cover and simmer for 2¼ to 2½ hours or until the duck is tender. Remove the duck, spoon surface fat from the liquid in the casserole, and keep the sauce hot.

Melt the remaining 3 tablespoons of butter in a separate skillet and fry the bread slices. Arrange the bread on a serving dish and spread with red currant jelly. Place the duck on top of the bread slices and spoon the sauce from the casserole over the duck. Serve with the remainder of the jelly as a condiment in a separate serving dish.

SERVES 4 TO 5.

*A dry Medoc fits this dish.*

# Kumquats and Stuffed Goose with Burgundy

On St. Martin's day in France a fat goose is always eaten for the festive meal. For centuries, the results of too much feasting has been called *Mal de Saint-Martin*.

> 1 goose (8 to 10 pounds), cleaned and prepared for roasting
> 1 teaspoon salt
> ½ teaspoon pepper
> 2 cloves garlic, minced
> 2 medium-sized onions, diced
> 1 teaspoon sage
> 2 tablespoons butter, softened
> 2¼ cups hot water
> 2 cups bread crumbs
> 1 cup Burgundy wine
> 2 dozen preserved kumquats

Rinse the goose inside and out with cold water, then dry thoroughly. Using a sharp fork, prick the skin all over the goose. Spread in the salt, pepper, and garlic.

To prepare the stuffing, mix the onions, sage, butter, and hot water with the bread crumbs. If the stuffing is too dry, add a little more hot water. Preheat the oven to 325°F.

Stuff the cavity of the goose, put the goose on a rack in a roasting pan, and bake for 1 hour. Remove the goose and rack, and drain the fat from the roasting pan. Raise the oven to 350°F. Return the rack and bird to the pan and continue cooking for 2½ hours. Remove the rack and bird once more and pour accumulated fat from the roasting pan. Return the goose to the pan, without the rack this time.

Pour the Burgundy over the goose and continue cooking at 350°F for another 30 minutes. Baste the goose frequently with the Burgundy in the pan. Ten minutes before the goose is done, add the kumquats to the pan. When the goose is done, remove to a serving platter and arrange the kumquats on both sides of the goose.

SERVES 4 TO 6.

*Serve with baked potatoes and a sparkling Burgundy.*

# Pheasant Normandy with Cream and Apples
*(Faisan Normand)*

> 2 pheasants (approximately 2 to 2½ pounds each),
>     cleaned and prepared for roasting
> 8 tablespoons butter
> 4 apples
> 1 cup Calvados
> ¼ teaspoon salt
> 3 dashes freshly ground pepper
> 1 pint heavy cream

Preheat the oven to 350°F. Heat 4 tablespoons of the butter in a heavy roasting pan or large earthenware *cocotte* on the top of the stove. Place the pheasants in the pan and brown on all sides over a moderate heat, approximately 10 minutes. Place the pan with the birds inside the oven and roast, covered, for 1 hour.

Near the end of the cooking time, peel, core, and slice the apples (not too thinly). Sauté the apple slices in the remaining butter until golden. Remove from heat.

Take the pheasant out of the oven and pour the juices from the roasting pan into a saucepan. Heat to boiling and add the Calvados, salt, and pepper. Ignite, shake gently, and let flame until it burns out. Add the heavy cream and stir over moderate heat until the sauce thickens.

Place the apples on the bottom of the roasting pan, around or under the pheasants. Pour the sauce over the birds. Lower the oven to 325°F and return the pheasants to the oven to cook until tender, approximately 10 minutes.

SERVES 4 TO 6.

*Serve with asparagus and Chateauneuf-de-Pape.*

# Simmered Rabbit
*(Lapin au Gratin)*

> 1 rabbit (2 to 2½ pounds), cut into serving-size
>   pieces
> Blood from the rabbit when it is cut into pieces.
>   Discard head, interior parts, giblets.
> 2 to 3 cups white wine
>   2 medium-sized onions, sliced into rings
>   ½ cup bacon fat
>   ½ tablespoon salt
>   ½ teaspoon pepper
>   ½ teaspoon basil
>   ½ teaspoon thyme
>   1 large bay leaf
>   ¼ cup (approximately) fresh white bread crumbs
>   1 clove garlic, minced
>   1 tablespoon parsley

When the butcher cuts up the rabbit, be sure he retains all the resulting blood. If you disjoint your rabbit at home, retain the blood in a bowl.

In a separate deep dish, pour in the wine and marinate the rabbit pieces for 2 hours in the wine. When ready to cook, sauté the onion rings in the bacon fat, then add the rabbit pieces. Brown the pieces on both sides and then season with the salt, pepper, basil, thyme, and bay leaf. Pour in the wine from the marinade and cover the pot. Simmer for approximately 1 hour or until the rabbit is cooked.

Make fresh white bread crumbs. It is important that these be made by rubbing pieces of bread between the palms of the hand. Commercial bread crumbs will not do. When the bread crumbs are ready, soak them in a bowl with the rabbit blood, as much as will be absorbed. Add the garlic and parsley.

Remove the rabbit pieces to a hot platter and keep hot in

the oven. Pour the bread mixture into the wine sauce in the pan and cook over a low heat for 5 minutes, stirring constantly. Pour the sauce over the rabbit pieces and serve.

SERVES 3 TO 4.

*A bright claret goes well with this dish.*

# Venison Stew with Red Wine
*(Cerf Daube au Vin Rouge)*

1 shoulder of venison (4 to 5 pounds)
1 cup port wine
½ cup wine vinegar
2 tablespoons salad oil
6 slices bacon
1 clove garlic, very finely minced
8 small carrots, cut into quarters
1 cup beef bouillon or broth
½ teaspoon salt
½ teaspoon pepper
½ teaspoon thyme
3 cloves garlic, left whole

In a large earthenware dish or large crock pot, prepare a marinade of the port, wine vinegar, and salad oil. Mix well. Place the venison in the marinade so that it is entirely covered. Increase the marinade in the same proportions if more is needed to cover. Marinate for at least 24 hours.

When ready to cook, remove the venison from the marinade, pour the marinade into a separate dish, and reserve. Fry the bacon slices in an oven-proof pot. When they are crisply done, take them out, break into small pieces, and set aside.

Dry the venison thoroughly with paper or cloth towels. Put it in the pot and brown well in the bacon fat on all sides. When the venison is thoroughly browned, lower the heat and spread the minced garlic over the top of the venison. Use the palms of your hands or the back of a spoon to press the garlic into the meat. Spread the bacon pieces on top.

Pour in the reserved marinade, cover, and cook for 30 minutes. Then add the carrots on all sides of the venison, along with the beef bouillon or broth. Season with the salt, pepper, and thyme and place the 3 whole garlic cloves in the pot on three sides. Cover again and cook in a 325°F oven for approximately 2 hours.

When the venison is done, strain the marinade mixture into a serving bowl and serve very hot along with the meat and carrots.

Serves 10 to 12.

*Accompany with a large dish of black or red currant jelly and a purée of buttered potatoes. A good, robust red wine goes well with this meal.*

# ∽5∾
# GERMANY AND THE LOW COUNTRIES

To some, Germany has achieved its greatest culinary fame as the land of the sausage. It has been said that Germany is the only place where the wurst is best and the best is wurst. Although the sausage may be a favored staple of *deutsches essen*, the cuisine of Germany has always been far more sophisticated and ingenuous than the sausage. Yet it is also true that German cuisine has been virtually untouched by French culinary influence.

It's true that Frederick II of Prussia became a culinary Francophile and insisted on only French dishes at his palace. Although the nobility of other German kingdoms imitated him, French influence went little further than the court. The German-speaking peoples did not, for the most part, respond to French culinary inroads. Vienna, jewel of the old Austro-Hungarian Empire, was quite alone in its embrace of French cuisine and French customs—so uniquely so that Goethe referred to the city as *eine kleine Paris*, a little Paris.

While the resistance to French culinary blandishments was not a conscious effort, it was very much the result of deep sociological and political factors. Cooking often followed conquest—the victors returning with new tastes, new ingredients, new gastronomic discoveries. There was little French conquest of Germany that lasted long enough to establish influence via that route. However, there were deeper resistances, anchored in the emotional and cultural genesis of the Germanic peoples. It must be remembered that French cuisine—which grew out of Italian cuisine, which in turn had Roman roots—was a development of essentially Latin peoples with Latin cultural and emotional affinities. The palate is not without its own psychological roots.

The Germans were a Teutonic people, originally a mixture of Viking tribes from the north. The original Teutons of the fourth century B.C. settled into northern and then Central Europe and joined with Slavic peoples who came later with a background of Asiatic blood. Through the years, the Latin influence played almost no part in this cultural development.

By the Middle Ages, German cooking in style and manner was rooted strongly in its own native foods, with Hungarian, Russian, and Slavic influences.

Today, when considering German cooking, we think of potatoes and sauerkraut as much as we do sausage, and rightly so. But the potato was not a major part of German cooking until the eighteenth century, and sauerkraut was unknown to Germans before the thirteenth century. Root vegetables, beets, turnips, parsnips, wheat, and rye were the basic ingredients of German dishes before the advent of cabbage. But the mainstay of German cooking was, and still is, pork, with the resulting eminence of the sausage. The old German states were filled with wild boars, and the ancestors of present-day farmers raised a variety of magnificent hogs. Westphalian *schinken* is still a prized variety of ham the world over. Milk cows were widespread, but beef cattle were hardly bred at all in Germany. Poultry and game played a part in German cuisine, but it was the pig that formed the main meat of the German *burgher*.

The sausage was one way in which variety was added to the consumption of pork, along with the normal problems of keeping meat fresh and edible. There are at least thirty widely popular varieties of German sausage today. But the sausage itself cannot be claimed as a German culinary original. Sausages are mentioned in Homer, and the Greek playwrights made numerous references to the sausage. Epicharmus, the author of Greek burlesque farces, wrote one called *Orya*, the Sausage. Aristophanes, in *The Clouds*, has a character implore: "Let them make sausages of me and serve me to the students."

The sausage in German cooking is a main dish of itself. It is often accompanied by potato salad, pickles, and wine, beer, or *schnapps* (whiskey). But it can be used in other recipes as well. A complete listing of the infinite varieties would be prohibitively voluminous, for almost every region had its own provincial versions. However, the following list can serve as a general guide to the types of sausage available and ways to prepare them.

BOCKWURST: Veal, cream or milk, eggs, parsley, chives, or onion. A delicate, white sausage. Cook for 10 minutes in scalding but not boiling water, then lightly brown in butter.

WEISSWURST: Veal, pork, sage, thyme, and parsley—the Bavarian cousin to the bockwurst. Simmer in butter for 5 minutes after immersing in scalding but not boiling water.

BRATWURST: Veal, pork, ginger, coriander, lemon rind, and mustard—a large sausage of Nürnberg origin. Simmer in beer or water for 10 minutes, then brown in small amount of butter or fat.

SCHWEINWURSTL: A small Bratwurst with more pork. Cook in the same manner, simmering for a slightly shorter time.

GERÄUCHERTE: A large, salami-sized bratwurst. Steam and slice. Serve hot or cold.

BERLINER BOCKWURST: Beef or beef and smoked pork; resembles a fat frankfurter. Fry in butter or boil in water for 7 to 10 minutes.

THURINGER WURST: Finely ground pork, and sometimes veal, dry milk solids, ginger, coriander, pepper, and ground celery seeds. Boil in water, grill, or fry in fat or butter.

FRANKFURTER: In Germany, beef or beef and pork. Bring water and frankfurters to a boil and then simmer for 5 minutes. They can also be fried in butter, broiled, or grilled.

KNACKWURST: Originated in Germany but has become very popular in the U.S. for soups, stews, and recipes using pork and beans. Usually pork and beef mixture. For kosher products only beef is used. Salt, pepper, and other ingredients added vary from maker to maker. Drop into boiling water and boil for 10 minutes.

SALAMI: Equal parts of coarsely cut beef and pork, white pepper, salt, garlic, and sugar. Serve cold, though slices may be heated and included in other dishes.

BIERWURST: Dry smoked salami made of chopped pork and beef, salt, black pepper, garlic, and sugar. Serve cold.

CERVELATWURST: The father of all cervelats. Equal parts of

coarse chopped beef and pork lightly seasoned with salt, pepper, sugar, and mustard. Serve cold.

BAUERNWURST: Smoked, coarsely ground pork and finely ground beef, sometimes bacon, pepper, and mace—the farmer's sausage. Steam, poach, and then fry or grill.

BLUTWURST: Blood sausage made of fresh pig's blood, pork, pork fat, and sometimes veal tongue. Place the wurst in boiling water, cover, and boil for 20 minutes. May also be thickly sliced and browned slowly in butter.

BRAUNSCHWEIGER: Smoked liver sausage made of pork liver and veal. Do not cook. Soft and spreadable; ready to eat.

BRAUNSCHWEIGER METTWURST: Same as braunschweiger but made with finely ground pork; ready to eat.

ZWEIBELWURST: Variation of braunschweiger with browned onions included; ready to eat.

FLEISCHWURST: Meat sausage of beef, pork, or both; lightly smoked. Serve hot or cold. If hot, steam, poach and slice thickly or fry thick slices in butter.

LEBERKÄSE: Loaf of pork, pork liver, bacon, eggs, and onion. Serve cold or slice thick and fry in butter and onion.

METTWURST: Different from braunschweiger mettwurst. Short and bright red. Made of three-quarters cured beef, one-quarter cured pork, ginger, allspice, mustard, coriander, and pepper.

JÄGDWURST: Hunter's sausage. Coarsely chopped pork and beef, salt, pepper, allspice, and finely ground pistachio nuts. Warm in the oven or serve cold.

But whether it was pork, sausages, game, or fowl, German cooking developed along its own lines and, in some strange manner, leapfrogged into Holland where Dutch burghers shared the same pleasure in food as did their German counterparts. That the natives of the Low Countries shared the Teutonic trencherman's gusto in dining can be seen in the paintings of Hals, Van Eyck, Rembrandt, Breughel, and Hieronymus Bosch. Indeed, German, Dutch, and Flemish cuisine is earthy, filling, satisfying in its own way. If, as has been said, French cuisine is the spirit of subtle, delicate dalliance in culinary terms, then German cooking is unadorned, sensual pleasure—the spirit of the bacchanalia rather than the boudoir. Of course, like all pleasures in this world, there is a time, a taste, and a joy for each.

# Boiled Beef
*(Gedampfes Rindfleisch)*

5 pounds boneless beef rump or brisket (second cut)
½ pound salt pork
  Cold water
4 carrots, cut into quarters
1 stalk celery, cut into 1-inch sections
3 medium-sized onions, cut into quarters
8 peppercorns
8 turnips, peeled and quartered
2 bay leaves

*Horseradish-Cream Sauce*

1 cup heavy cream
2 tablespoons sugar
½ teaspoon lemon juice
5 tablespoons horseradish, grated

In a large pot, place the beef and salt pork and add enough cold water to cover. Boil the water for 5 minutes, then lower the heat. Add all the other ingredients and simmer, covered, for 3 to 4 hours or until the beef is tender.

Remove the meat and keep warm in the oven. Strain the broth and reserve the vegetables. Let the broth cool for 10 to 15 minutes or until the fat has risen to the top. Skim off the fat and reheat the broth.

Place the vegetables around the beef and salt pork on a serving dish and pour the heated broth over all. Serve with Horseradish-Cream Sauce in a separate dish.

To prepare the Horseradish-Cream Sauce, whip the cream. Blend all the ingredients thoroughly with the whipped cream, using a blender if you desire.

Makes slightly over 1 cup of sauce.

SERVES 6 TO 8.

# Bavarian Pickled Beef
*(Sauerbraten Bayrischer)*

4 to 5 pounds boneless beef shoulder
2½ cups water
5 cups beer
1 bay leaf
1 onion, sliced
1 lemon, cut into quarters
1 tomato, chopped
6 peppercorns
3 tablespoons butter
1¼ tablespoons sugar
1 lemon, thinly sliced
1 cup sour cream

Make a marinade of the water, beer, bay leaf, onion, lemon (quartered), tomato, and peppercorns. Place the meat in a large pan, cover with the marinade, and refrigerate for 2 days.

When ready to cook, remove the meat from the marinade and dry. Strain the marinade and reserve in a separate bowl. Brown the meat in butter on all sides. When browned, add 1½ cups of the strained marinade along with the sugar and sliced lemon. Mix well and cook over a medium heat for 2½ hours or until the meat is tender.

Remove the meat from the pan. Take the fat off the top of the liquid in the pan and add the sour cream. Mix thoroughly and reheat carefully so that the cream does not curdle. To serve, slice the meat first and pour the sauce over it.

SERVES 6.
*Serve with red cabbage only.*

# Braised Beef Liver
*(Geschmorte Rindsleber)*

> 1 pound beef liver, cut into strips 1 inch wide and
>     1/4 to 1/2 inch thick
> 1 cup milk
> 1/2 teaspoon salt
> 1/4 cup flour
> 3 tablespoons salad oil
> 1 medium-sized onion, minced
> 2 cups beef bouillon
> 1 tablespoon lemon juice
> 2 tablespoons sugar
> 1/4 cup sour cream

Have the butcher prepare the strips of liver. Immerse the strips in the milk in a pan for at least 1 hour. Remove from the milk and set aside. Discard the milk. Blend the salt into the flour and dredge the liver strips with the mixture. Sauté the strips in the oil in a pan until browned on both sides and remove. Put the onion into the pan, cook for a few minutes until it begins to soften, and then sprinkle over the liver strips with a spoon.

Pour the beef bouillon, lemon juice, and sugar into the pan. Return the liver strips and simmer gently for 10 minutes. Remove from heat and stir in the sour cream until blended.

SERVES 4.

*Serve with buttered Brussels sprouts and mashed potatoes.*

# City of Leyden Hotpot
*(Leyden Hutsepot)*

In the sixteenth century, when the Dutch revolted against Spain, the Dutch city of Leyden was under heavy siege. All provisions were cut off. The traditional *hutsepot* became a community dish, with everyone contributing whatever they could. This version is still served at the October commemoration of that time of trial.

        4 pounds beef brisket or flanken
          Salted water
        2 sausages, frankfurters, bockwurst, or bratwurst
        6 small onions, diced
        6 potatoes, peeled and cut into small cubes
        8 carrots, diced
        ½ cup chicken fat
        ½ tablespoon salt
        ½ teaspoon pepper
        ½ teaspoon cayenne pepper

Put the meat in a large pot and add enough lightly salted water to cover. Simmer over a low heat for 1½ hours. Add the sausages and vegetables. Simmer for 30 minutes or until the vegetables are soft enough to mash.

Remove the meat and sausages and drain the broth into a bowl. Mash the vegetables and add the chicken fat, stirring until the mixture is smooth. Add the seasonings and blend well. Remove the outer casings from the sausages. Slice the sausages thinly and fold into the vegetable mixture. Heat over a low flame. Slice the meat and lay it over the vegetable mixture. Heat the reserved broth and serve separately as a sauce.

SERVES 8.

# Stuffed Head of Cabbage
*(Gefullter Krautkopf)*

> ¾ pound beef chuck, ground
> ½ pound veal, ground
> ¼ pound pork, ground
> 1 cup bread crumbs
> 1 onion, finely chopped
> 1 clove garlic, minced
> 1 teaspoon oregano
> ¾ tablespoon salt
> ½ teaspoon pepper
> 1 large head cabbage
>   Water
> 2 tablespoons butter
> 1 cup bouillon
> 2 teaspoons caraway seeds

Preheat the oven to 350°F. Mix the 3 meats together and combine with the bread crumbs, onion, garlic, oregano, salt, and pepper. Set aside.

Place the head of cabbage in a large pot. Add enough water to cover, bring to a boil, and then simmer for 5 minutes. Remove cabbage leaves one by one until you have 10 large ones that are limp enough to roll yet still retain a certain firmness. Place the meatloaf mixture evenly into each cabbage leaf, roll up the leaf, and tuck in the ends.

In a baking dish, melt the butter and add ½ cup of the bouillon. Place the cabbage rolls in the dish and sprinkle each one with the caraway seeds. Bake for 30 minutes, then add the remaining bouillon. Continue baking for another 30 minutes. Add more if needed.

SERVES 5 TO 6.

# Beef Tongue and Madeira
*(Ochsenzunge und Madeira)*

    1 beef tongue
      Water
    1 tablespoon salt
    2 carrots, cut into cubes
    2 stalks celery
    6 peppercorns
    4 sprigs parsley
    1 bay leaf
    1 cup beef gravy
    ½ cup Madeira wine
    ½ teaspoon thyme

In a large pot, add enough cold water to cover the tongue, sprinkle in the salt, and boil for 5 minutes. Reduce the heat and simmer for 45 minutes. Add the carrots, celery, peppercorns, parsley, and bay leaf and continue cooking for another 2 hours.

When the tongue is done, the outer skin should pull off easily. Remove the tongue, skin it, and set aside. Strain the stock and reserve. In a separate saucepan, combine the beef gravy, Madeira, thyme, and 1 cup of the stock. Bring to a boil, then lower the heat and simmer gently until the sauce thickens and reduces.

Slice the tongue and pour the sauce over the meat.

SERVES 6 TO 8.

# Viennese-style Veal Cutlets
*(Wiener Schnitzel)*

Few people know that the Celts founded Vienna and that this city later became a major Roman military base. Centuries later, it was the seat of the Hapsburg Empire. Few people do not know that Vienna is the home of the Strauss waltzes and the wonderful *Wiener Schnitzel*—so much for the impact of history versus art and appetite.

> 6 large veal cutlets, pounded thin
> 6 tablespoons lemon juice
> 1 tablespoon salt
> 1 teaspoon pepper
> ½ cup flour
> 3 eggs
> 3 tablespoons cold water
> 1½ cups bread crumbs
> 4 tablespoons butter
> 2 tablespoons salad oil
> 6 very thin slices lemon
> 6 capers

Have the butcher pound the cutlets thin, but not as thin as for scallopini. Sprinkle the cutlets with the lemon juice on both sides and let them soak for 30 minutes. Then season the cutlets with the salt and pepper.

Dust the cutlets lightly with the flour on both sides. In a bowl, beat the eggs with the cold water. Dip the cutlets into the egg mixture, coating them lightly, and then dredge them with the bread crumbs. Let the cutlets stand at room temperature for 30 minutes or chill them for 15 minutes in the refrigerator.

Heat the butter and oil in a skillet but do not allow the butter to burn. Fry the cutlets in the skillet over a moderate heat, turning at least once, so that both sides become golden, approximately 5 minutes per side. If the skillet cannot hold

6 cutlets at once, keep the cooked ones in a heated oven until the others are ready. When ready to serve, place a lemon slice on each cutlet and 1 caper in the center of each lemon slice.

SERVES 6.

*A May wine goes well with Wiener Schnitzel.*

# Berlin All-in-One Pot
*(Berliner Eintopf)*

½ pound pork loin, cubed
½ pound beef chuck, cubed
½ pound veal shoulder, cubed
3 tablespoons butter
2 medium-sized onions, sliced
2 cups beef bouillon
2 medium-sized carrots, cut into eighths
6 pieces cabbage, cut into wedges
1 teaspoon dry mustard
3 potatoes, peeled and diced into small cubes
½ teaspoon salt
½ teaspoon pepper

Melt the butter in a large pot. Add the pork, beef, and veal and brown thoroughly, stirring frequently. Reduce the heat and simmer for 10 minutes. Add the onions and cook gently for another 5 minutes.

Add the bouillon, carrots, cabbage, and mustard. Stir and cook for 5 minutes. Then add the potatoes, season with the salt and pepper, cover, and simmer for 30 minutes. Add more bouillon if necessary.

SERVES 4.

*Serve out of the pot, along with or atop buttered noodles, along with a Moselle.*

# Silesian Heavenly Bounty
*(Schlesisches Himmelreich)*

> 1½ pounds pork shoulder or loin, cut into 1-inch cubes
> ½ pound dried apples, cut into rough cubes
> ½ pound dried prunes, pitted
> ¼ pound dried apricots
>   Water
> ¼ teaspoon salt
>   6 tablespoons butter
> 1½ tablespoons cornstarch
> ½ teaspoon ground cloves
> ½ teaspoon sugar

Preheat the oven to 300°F. Simmer the dried fruit in water (or according to package directions) until it softens. In a casserole, melt half the butter and add the salt and pork cubes. Brown the meat on all sides. Drain the softened fruit through a fine strainer and reserve the liquid. Stir the fruit into the casserole with the browned meat.

In a separate skillet, melt the rest of the butter and add the cornstarch and liquid drained from the fruit. Cook until mixture thickens. Add the cloves and sugar and pour the sauce into the casserole. Bake for at least 30 minutes or until the pork is tender.

SERVES 4 TO 6.

*Potatoes, mashed and buttered, are often served with this dish, along with a Rhine wine.*

# Rib of Pork
*(Kasseler Rippchen)*

1 center loin pork rib roast (5 to 6 pounds)
2 medium-sized onions, sliced into rings
2 tomatoes, thickly sliced
3 cups boiling water
2 tablespoons butter
2 tablespoons flour
½ teaspoon salt
¾ cup sour cream

Preheat the oven to 350°F. Layer the bottom of a roasting pan with the onions and tomatoes and place the roast over them. Bake, covered, for 30 minutes. Add 1½ cups of the boiling water and continue baking for another 30 minutes. Then add the remainder of the boiling water and continue cooking, covered, for 1 hour more.

Remove the meat. Strain the liquid in the pan and reserve. Add the butter to the scrapings on the bottom of the pan and melt. Add the flour and mix together over a moderate heat until the mixture begins to bubble. Slowly add the strained liquid from the pan, along with the salt. Stir until smooth. Lower the heat and stir in the sour cream. Let the sour cream heat, but do not boil. Pour the sauce over the sliced roast and serve.

SERVES 10.

*Potatoes with chives make a good balance, along with a Moselle.*

# Sour Cream and Pork Chops
*(Saurer Sahne und Schweinskotelett)*

During a terrible plague in 1517, in which the people of Munich were afraid to drink the city's water, the apprentice butchers leaped into the fountain in the center of Munich to show that the water was safe to touch and use. The *Metzgersprung*, or butchers' leap, is still commemorated every three years by the butchers of Munich.

On the day of the celebration, before the fountain, the master butcher asks the apprentices if they know what an honor it is to belong to the ancient, most loyal and honorable guild of butchers and if they are ready to prove themselves worthy of the privileges accorded to them. When all the questions have been answered, toasts are drunk, and the apprentice butchers leap into the fountain. After the *Metzgersprung*, the apprentices receive a white cloth to be tied around their necks and a silver medal as a symbolic reward for their courage.

        4 loin or rib pork chops, 1 inch thick
        3 tablespoons butter
        ½ teaspoon salt
        3 tablespoons flour
        ½ cup chicken bouillon
        1 tablespoon tomato paste
        1 cup sour cream

In a skillet, melt the butter and sauté the chops, browning thoroughly on each side. Remove the chops from the skillet and add the salt and flour, stirring thoroughly. Slowly add the chicken bouillon, tomato paste, and sour cream, stirring constantly over a low heat until the mixture is smooth. (Keep the heat low or the sour cream will curdle.) Return the chops to the skillet and simmer, uncovered, for 15 to 20 minutes or until done.

SERVES 4.

*Add a cold Riesling to the meal.*

# Pork Rolls
*(Schweinsrouladen)*

    6 boneless pork steaks, cut from the top shoulder
    1 tablespoon salt
    1 teaspoon pepper
    3 tablespoons flour
    2 medium-sized onions, finely chopped
    6 slices bacon, diced
    1 cup raisins
    1 cup crushed pineapple
    3 tablespoons butter
    1½ cups Rhine wine

Have the butcher cut the 6 steaks, removing the bone and trimming all the fat from the edges. Season each steak with the salt and pepper, then sprinkle with the flour on both sides. Pound the steaks thin and press in the salt, pepper, and flour using wax paper and a pounding tool or the bottom of a pan. Set aside.

In a pan, cook the onions and bacon until the onions are soft and the bacon bits are crisp. Remove the pan from the heat, add the raisins and crushed pineapple, and stir. Spread the mixture thinly across the pork steaks, roll each one up, and tie or fasten tightly with skewers. Melt the butter in the pan and brown the rolled pork steaks on all sides. Pour the wine in and simmer, covered, for approximately 15 to 25 minutes or until the meat is tender.

SERVES 3 TO 6.

# Pork Pot Roast with Beer
*(Schweinfleisch in Bier)*

    1 pork shoulder or Boston butt (about 5 pounds)
      Water
    6 large carrots, cut into quarters
   12 small white onions
      Turnips, cut into eighths
    2 bay leaves
    1 tablespoon salt
    6 peppercorns
    1 tablespoon sugar
    1 pint, 6 ounces beer
    2 cups hard, stale bread crumbs, from pumpernickel
      or black bread

Place the pork in a large pot, add enough cold water to
cover, and boil for 10 minutes. Remove from the heat and
pour off the water. Then add 3 cups of fresh water. Cook,
covered, over a moderate heat for 1 hour, then add the vegetables, seasonings, sugar, and beer. Continue cooking for
another 2 hours.

Preheat the oven to 350°F. Remove the meat from the pot,
strain the broth and reserve, and set the vegetables aside.
Let the broth chill for 30 minutes, then skim the fat from the
surface. Put the meat, fat side up, in a roasting pan, add the
vegetables, and roast for 30 minutes until the fat is crisped
and browned. Add the bread crumbs to the broth and stir in
well until the broth is thickened. Remove the roasting pan
from the oven and place over a moderate heat to do this.

Pour the juice into a gravy boat and serve over sliced meat
with the vegetables.

SERVES 6.

*Potato pancakes make a nice side dish along with a hearty
beer.*

# Pears, Beans, and Bacon
*(Birnen, Bohnen, und Speck)*

Teutonic mythology dictated that a flitch of bacon, *Speck-seite*, be offered to the god Percunnos during thunderstorms. Superstitious farmers used to carry a slab of bacon into the fields during thunderstorms. If the storm ended without real damage to their crops or homes, they would take the bacon back and eat it with their families as a symbolic sacrifice.

    8 slices bacon, not too thin
    ¾ cup water
    8 pears, peeled and sliced
    2 thin slivers lemon peel
    1 pound green beans, cut into halves or thirds
    1 teaspoon salt
    ¼ cup sugar
    1 teaspoon lemon juice
    1 tablespoon white vinegar

Heat the water in a saucepan and add the pear slices and lemon peel. Bring to a boil, then lower the heat and simmer for 10 minutes. Add the beans and salt to the saucepan and continue simmering. In a separate skillet, fry the bacon until it is crisp. Remove the bacon and drain. Add the sugar, lemon juice, and white vinegar to the bacon fat in the skillet and mix. Cook for 2 minutes and pour into the saucepan containing the pears and beans. Cook over a low heat until the beans are tender. Crumble the bacon into bits, add to the skillet, and stir thoroughly.

SERVES 4 TO 6.

*Serve with buttered toast on the side.*

# Sausage in Beer
*(Bratwurst in Bier)*

18 bratwurst
Boiling water, enough to cover
2 tablespoons butter
½ teaspoon pepper
1½ cups beer
½ tablespoon arrowroot
½ teaspoon salt

In a skillet, cover the sausages with boiling water, cook for 3 to 4 minutes, and drain. Melt the butter in a skillet and brown the sausages on all sides. Remove from the heat and drain off the fat. Sprinkle the pepper over the sausages, add the beer to the skillet, and simmer over a low heat for 15 to 20 minutes or until almost done. Mix the arrowroot in and thicken the beer sauce, stirring well. Add the salt and continue stirring, but do not thicken the sauce too much.

SERVES 6.

*Serve with mashed, peppered, and buttered potatoes on the side.*

# Bremen Meat Salad
*(Bremer Fleischsalat)*

> ½ pound boiled ham, cut into thin strips
> 3 frankfurters, diced
> 1 bierwurst, diced
> 4 sweet gherkins, diced
> 2 tablespoons wine vinegar
> ½ tablespoon salt
> ½ teaspoon pepper
> ½ cup mayonnaise
> 4 leaves lettuce, cut into small sections

Combine all the ingredients in a salad bowl, mixing very thoroughly.

SERVES 4.

*Serve over whole lettuce leaves.*

# Hunter's Hen
*(Jager Huhn)*

    1 broiler or frying chicken (3 to 4 pounds), cut into
        serving-size pieces
    ½ tablespoon salt
    ½ teaspoon pepper
    ½ teaspoon paprika
    2 tablespoons butter
    2 tablespoons salad oil
    ½ pound button mushrooms
    4 scallions, finely chopped
    ½ cup Rhine wine
    1 tablespoon brandy

Coat the chicken pieces with a mixture of the salt, pepper, and paprika. In a large skillet, melt the butter and the oil together. Put the chicken pieces in the skillet and brown well on both sides over a medium heat until the skin begins to crisp, about 15 to 20 minutes.

Remove the chicken pieces and keep warm in a heated oven. Add the mushrooms and scallions to the skillet and sauté until softened. Then add the wine and brandy, stir well, and heat. Return the chicken pieces to the skillet, simmer for another 30 minutes, and serve, pouring the sauce over the pieces.

SERVES 4.

# Rabbit in Pepper
(*Hasenpfeffer*)

        1 rabbit, cut into serving-size pieces
        1 cup red wine
        ½ cup water
        ½ cup wine vinegar
        1 medium-sized onion, sliced
        ½ tablespoon salt
        3 bay leaves
        4 whole cloves
        2 tablespoons flour
        2 tablespoons butter
        1 small onion, finely chopped
        ¼ teaspoon thyme
        ¼ teaspoon tarragon
        12 peppercorns
        1 tablespoon lemon rind, grated

In a large pan, make a marinade of the red wine, water, wine vinegar, sliced onion, salt, bay leaves, and cloves. Marinate the rabbit pieces for 24 hours.

When ready to cook, remove the pieces, reserving the marinade, pat dry, and dust with the flour. Sauté the rabbit in a skillet in the butter, browning until the pieces are crisp on all sides. Remove the rabbit pieces to another pot and pour the fat out of the skillet. Pour the marinade into the skillet, along with the chopped onion, thyme, tarragon, peppercorns, and grated lemon rind. Mix well and pour over the rabbit pieces in the pot. Cover and simmer over a low heat until tender, approximately 30 to 45 minutes.

Remove the rabbit pieces to a serving platter. Drain the sauce and pour over the meat.

SERVES 4.

*Serve with spaetzle and a good Moselle.*

# Pheasant and Sauerkraut with Wine
*(Fasan und Weinkraut)*

It may shock many people to learn that, ornithologically, a chicken is a pheasant. However, in taste the pheasant is as far away as it is in beauty. Although domestic pheasant may be used for this dish, wild pheasant is recommended.

> 1 pheasant (3 to 3½ pounds)
> ½ tablespoon salt
> ½ teaspoon pepper
> 2 strips bacon
> 2 large onions, chopped
> 4 tablespoons butter
> 2½ pounds sauerkraut
> 1 cup beef bouillon
> 1 cup white wine
> 1 large potato, peeled and grated

Bring the bird to room temperature and rub it inside and out with the salt and pepper. (If you are using wild pheasant, the bird should be hung for 2 to 6 days, preferably at your butcher's.) Preheat the oven to 400°F.

Wrap the bacon strips over the breast. Place the pheasant in a large and shallow terrine or casserole and brown it in the oven for 15 minutes.

In a separate skillet, sauté the onions in the butter until softened. In a colander, rinse the sauerkraut with warm water and add it to the sautéed onions. Cover and simmer over a low heat for 10 minutes.

Remove the pheasant from the terrine or casserole and add the beef bouillon. Stir well, then pour half of the bouillon over the sauerkraut. Add the wine and the grated potato to the sauerkraut and stir well over a low heat. Then line the entire terrine with the sauerkraut and the liquid. Place the pheasant back on top of the sauerkraut and bake in a 375°F oven for 45 minutes or until the bird is tender. Baste the pheasant frequently with the pan juices.

Serve the pheasant with the sauerkraut. Drain off the juices and serve separately in a gravy boat.

SERVES 3 TO 4.

*A very cold Johannisberger is proper with this dish.*

# JEWISH COOKING

THE very words, *Jewish Cooking*, can bring on a spirited debate. Some say that there is no such thing, that Jewish cooking is the most international of all cuisines. Others claim it is the most traditional. In one sense, Jewish cooking is truly international, for at the time of the *Diaspora* Jewish people migrated to almost every country. Their cooking, just as their language and existence, took on the flavor and the character of the countries they settled in.

Yet the very heart of Jewish cooking—those dishes that were part of the religious and cultural history of the Jewish people—remained untouched. These were not simply traditional dishes but a cuisine inextricably bound up with the existence of a people and a faith. That essence is no less so today. These dishes, and all that surrounds them, are the real Jewish cooking, whether they are part of a joyful or a solemn occasion. To echo the *seder*, this is what makes Jewish cuisine different from all other cuisines. These dishes are a culinary record of the trials and triumphs of a people and can truly be called a cuisine of commemoration.

The *knaidlach*, dumplings of *matzo*, symbolize in certain Passover rites the round stones that Moses flung against the Egyptian wall holding his people prisoner in Egypt. The *matzo* itself recalls the unleavened dough the Israelites baked as they fled across the desert. In Eastern Europe in particular, *blintzes*, always a part of the spring Shavouth celebration, were filled with cheese to commemorate the time when the Jews returned from Mount Sinai to find that the milk in their jugs had turned sour. The *holishkes*—rolled chopped meat cooked in grape leaves, traditionally part of the Sukkoth harvest time—symbolize the vineyards of the ancient Palestine hillsides. The fruits of the German Jew's *strudel* recall the fruits of the harvest. The triangular shape of the Purim *hamantaschen* cookies are each a little reminder of the hat worn by the evil King Haman and Esther's victory over him. In Central Europe, *latkes*, or potato pancakes, were always part of the Hanukkah—the oil in which they were fried symbolizing the oil found by the Maccabees when they recaptured Jerusalem from the Greeks after 2,000 years.

The meanings are intrinsic to Jewish cooking. All the rest, the borrowed national touches, are embroidery only. The dietary laws, the ancient taboos, were for the most part derived from practical and hygienic wisdoms, often given a religious significance to insure acceptance and compliance. Many of these ancient guidelines have been recognized as unnecessary for modern living by numbers of Jewish people today. Others maintain them as a matter of faith and as a reminder of how close yesterday still is in the span of history.

As we have seen, climate and conquests, geography and sociology, and culture and politics have all influenced the development of most cuisines, but Jewish cuisine is the only one rooted in the spiritual essence of a people. Today we can all share in the pleasures of those dishes and remember Elijah who, arising at the angel's touch in the wilderness, "did eat and drink and went in the strength of that meat forty days and forty nights" (1 Kings 19:8).

# Cholent

Biblical law forbids cooking on the Jewish sabbath, so for strict observers, food has to be prepared for Friday night and Saturday and kept on a lighted fire. (It is against the law to strike a match on the sabbath.) Cholent is ideal for any time when a large dish must be prepared ahead of time.

>  4 pounds beef chuck, flanken, or brisket
>  1 veal marrow bone
>  3 large onions, sliced
>  4 tablespoons chicken fat
>  8 medium-sized potatoes, peeled and cut into
>      quarters
>  1 cup dried lima beans
>  1 cup barley
>  1 teaspoon salt
>  ½ teaspoon pepper
>  1 clove garlic, minced
>  ¼ teaspoon paprika
>  1½ tablespoons flour
>      Boiling water
>  1 bay leaf

Preheat the oven to 325°F. In a large iron kettle or heavy cooking pot, sauté the onions in the chicken fat until golden. Place the meat and marrow bone in the center of the pot over the sautéed onions and surround with potatoes, lima beans, and barley.

Mix the salt, pepper, garlic, and paprika with the flour and sprinkle over everything. Pour boiling water slowly over the meat until it is covered with ½ inch to spare. Add the bay leaf. Cover tightly and bake for 4 hours. Keep in a warm oven on the very lowest heat until ready to use.

SERVES 6 TO 8.

# Stuffed Cabbage

    1½ pounds beef chuck or round, ground twice
    1 large head cabbage
      Boiling water
    ¾ cup cooked rice
    ½ cup tomato juice
    1 teaspoon salt
    1 can (8 ounces) whole tomatoes
    ¼ cup brown sugar
    ½ cup raisins
      Almonds, blanched and halved
    1 teaspoon lemon juice
    6 ginger snaps
    ½ cup water

Use only the large outer leaves of the cabbage. There should be at least 12 of these. Place them in boiling water until they are wilted, approximately 10 minutes. Remove and drain on paper towels. Trim the thick center rib off the leaves.

Thoroughly mix the ground meat with the rice, tomato juice, and salt. Place a tablespoon of the mixture into each cabbage leaf, roll up, and tuck in the ends to seal.

In a large pot, place the whole tomatoes, brown sugar, raisins, almonds, lemon juice, and ginger snaps. Let simmer for 10 minutes. Add ½ cup of water and place the stuffed cabbage leaves into the pot. Simmer over a low heat for 1 to 1½ hours. Baste occasionally with the sauce in the pot. The sauce may be poured over the leaves when serving.

SERVES 6.

# Purim Potpourri

Purim celebrates the victory of Queen Esther over Haman, a Persian official who plotted to destroy the Jewish people. It is a joyful celebration of feasting and dancing. On Purim eve, the children gather to listen to the megillah of Esther, the story that tells how she and her Uncle Mordecai saved her people.

Even the Purim stews have a particularly joyful flavor, as in this dish.

    1 brisket of beef (4 to 5 pounds), cut into strips first,
        then the strips cut into halves
    ½ pound dried prunes
    1 orange, sliced with the rind
    ½ lemon, sliced with the rind
    ¼ pound apricots (soak first if using dried)
    ½ cup apricot brandy
    1 teaspoon salt
    1 tablespoon salad oil
    2 medium-sized onions, diced
    ¾ cup beef broth
    ½ teaspoon cinnamon
        Dash of nutmeg
    ½ cup honey
    4 sweet potatoes, peeled and cut into quarters

In a deep dish, put the prunes, orange slices, lemon slices, apricots, and brandy. Let soak a minimum of 2 hours.

When ready to begin cooking, sprinkle the salt over the meat. In a large pan, heat the oil, put in the onions, and cook for 10 minutes. Then add the meat and brown on all sides. Pour in the beef broth, cover, and cook over a moderate heat for 45 minutes. Add the cinnamon and nutmeg and stir well, then pour in the fruit and brandy mixture. Add the honey and mix thoroughly. Cover and continue cooking for 35 more minutes.

Add the sweet potatoes to the pot, stir, cover, and continue cooking for another 45 minutes.

SERVES 8.

*A Rose of Carmel wine goes well with this festive dish.*

# Yemenite Soup

Yemen was once part of the ancient kingdom of Sheba, which figured in the spice trade of Africa, India, and Europe. Yemenite Jews brought their love of spices with them wherever they went. Here is one of their unusual soup recipes.

1½ pounds beef chuck, cubed
5 cups beef bouillon
3 tablespoons salad oil
5 cloves garlic, minced
½ teaspoon coriander seed
3 stalks celery, chopped
2 tomatoes, cut into small pieces
1 tablespoon salt
1 teaspoon pepper
5 whole cardamom seeds

In a pot, heat the bouillon and add the meat. Cook over a moderate heat for 30 minutes. In a separate skillet, heat the oil and sauté the garlic, coriander, celery, and tomatoes. Sauté for approximately 5 minutes, then pour the mixture into the pot with the meat. Season with the salt and pepper and put in the cardamom seeds. Stir well and continue to cook, stirring frequently, over a low heat for another 15 to 30 minutes or until the beef cubes are tender.

SERVES 4 TO 5.

# Tzimmes

2 pounds boneless chuck beef, cut into 1-inch cubes
12 carrots
2 small onions, sliced
3 tablespoons chicken fat
½ tablespoon salt
4 white potatoes, peeled and sliced
4 sweet potatoes, peeled and sliced
¾ pound dried prunes
3 cups cold water
¼ cup honey
1 cup tomato juice
¼ cup brown sugar
3 tablespoons sugar

Cut the carrots lengthwise into quarters, then cut the strips into 2-inch sections. In a large kettle, sauté the carrot strips in the chicken fat, turning frequently. When they begin to soften, add the onion slices and sauté another 5 minutes. Then add the salt.

Put a thick layer of beef cubes on top of the carrots and onions, followed by a layer of the white potatoes, one of prunes, and one of sweet potatoes. Continue layering until all the beef cubes, potatoes, and prunes have been used.

Stir 1¼ cups of water, the honey, tomato juice, and brown sugar together and add to the kettle. Simmer over a low heat for 1 hour. Preheat the oven to 375°F.

In a separate saucepan, mix ¼ cup of the water with the sugar and heat over a high flame until the sugar thickens and begins to carmelize. Pour the remaining water over the carmelized sugar and add to the kettle. Place in the oven for 2¼ hours.

SERVES 6.

# Passover Meatloaf

The following dish is for Passover meals, when time, effort, and economy make themselves felt.

> 1 pound beef chuck or round, ground
> 1 pound veal shoulder, ground
> 2 medium-sized onions, minced
> 2 medium-sized potatoes, grated
> 1 teaspoon salt
> ½ teaspoon pepper
> ¾ cup water
> ½ cup chicken fat
> 3 hard-boiled eggs

Preheat the oven to 350°F. In a mixing bowl, mix the onions and potatoes with the meat. Add the salt, pepper, and water and mix everything thoroughly. Warm a loaf pan in the oven, then grease it well with the chicken fat. Pour half of the meat mixture into the pan, smoothing it out to the corners. Press the hard-boiled eggs lightly into the meat in a row lengthwise along the pan. Cover with the remainder of the meat. Bake for approximately 45 minutes to 1 hour. Slice and serve hot.

SERVES 4 TO 6.

# Fry Beef Roll

¾ pound beef chuck or round, ground
8 slices kosher fry beef (very thin slices of pastrami
   may be substituted)
1 egg
¾ cup matzo meal or crumbs
½ tablespoon salt
½ teaspoon pepper
½ teaspoon paprika
½ teaspoon garlic salt

Mix the ground beef with the egg, matzo meal or crumbs, salt, pepper, paprika, and garlic salt. Lay the slices of fry beef or pastrami out on a sheet of waxed paper, overlapping each slice slightly. Spread the ground beef mixture over the slices and roll up as you would a jelly roll. Wrap in the waxed paper and refrigerate for 2 hours, until the roll is firmly set. Cut into slices about 1 inch thick, using a sharp knife. Broil approximately 10 minutes on each side.

SERVES 3 TO 4.

*Serve with mashed potatoes and string beans.*

# Beef Eggplant

1¼ pounds beef chuck, ground
1 medium-sized eggplant
2 tablespoons salt
4 tablespoons salad oil
1 egg
1 medium-sized onion, diced
¼ tablespoon salt
½ teaspoon pepper
1 can (8 ounces) tomato sauce

Peel and slice the eggplant and spread with the 2 table-spoons of salt. Set aside to drain for approximately 1 hour. After the eggplant drains, rinse off the salt and pat the eggplant dry with paper towels. In a skillet, heat the oil, brown the eggplant slices on both sides, and remove to paper towels to drain.

Preheat the oven to 350°F. Thoroughly mix the ground beef with the egg, onion, salt, and pepper. In a flat oven-proof dish, arrange 4 slices of eggplant. Spread a layer of meat over each of the slices, then coat the meat with a thin layer of tomato sauce. Repeat the layers of eggplant, meat, and to-mato sauce until everything is used, or 3 to 4 layers of each. Bake for 45 minutes to 1 hour.

SERVES 4.

*Serve with sliced carrots.*

# Applesauce Meatballs

1½ pounds beef chuck or round, ground
¾ cup cornflakes
1 small onion, minced
¼ teaspoon salt
Dash of garlic powder
1 egg, beaten
½ cup applesauce
1 can (15 ounces) tomato sauce

Preheat the oven to 350°F. Crush the cornflakes into small bits with a wooden spoon. In a large bowl, mix all the ingredients together except the tomato sauce. Shape the mixed ingredients into small meatballs and place in an uncovered roasting pan. Pour the tomato sauce over the meatballs and bake 45 minutes to 1 hour.

SERVES 4.

# Liver Cutlets
*(Leberschnitzel)*

> 1¼ pounds beef liver
> 1 large onion, cut into quarters
> 1 large potato, peeled
> 2 eggs
> ½ teaspoon salt
> ¼ teaspoon pepper
> 4 tablespoons matzo meal or crumbs
> 4 tablespoons salad oil

In a grinder or food processor, grind the potato and onion. Broil the liver lightly, cut it into quarters, and add to the grinder or processor. Grind with the onion and potato. Remove the liver mixture and mix in a bowl with the eggs, salt, pepper, and matzo meal or crumbs.

Mold into 8 patties and fry in the oil in a skillet, browning both sides well. Remove and drain on paper towels.

SERVES 4.

*Serve with Brussels sprouts and a very cold dry white wine.*

# Stuffed Veal Breast I

Passover is the celebration of that time when the angel of death "passed over" the houses of the Israelites, which were marked as Moses had commanded, and when they were delivered out of Egypt. It is the holiday richest in symbolism of the table, and the main dish of the first *seder* is always something special. Only unleavened ingredients are used, in memory of the unleavened dough the Israelites used as they crossed the desert.

    1 breast of veal (6 to 8 pounds)
    8 matzos, crumbled
    ½ cup water
    3 eggs, beaten
    ½ teaspoon parsley, chopped
    3 tablespoons onion, chopped
    ¼ cup potato starch
    ¾ teaspoon salt
    ¼ teaspoon pepper
    2 sprigs dill weed, chopped
    ½ teaspoon ginger
    6 tablespoons chicken fat
    1 onion, sliced
    ¼ cup boiling water

Have the butcher prepare the breast of veal for stuffing. The breast bones between the ribs should be cracked but left on to supply the juices needed. A large pocket should be made in the veal, extending across the width of the breast.

In a bowl, sprinkle the crumbled matzos with the ½ cup of water and add the eggs, parsley, and chopped onion. Mix the ingredients well. Stuff the mixture into the pocket of the veal, packing firmly. Secure the pocket with small skewers or sew with heavy thread.

Preheat the oven to 500°F. Mix the potato starch with the salt, pepper, dill, and ginger. Dredge the stuffed veal with this mixture. Put the chicken fat, sliced onion, and boiling water in a roasting pan. Roast, turning until browned, and then reduce the heat to 300°F. Cover and cook slowly until tender, approximately 2½ hours. Remove the cover during the last 15 minutes to brown the veal.

SERVES 6 TO 9.

*Serve on a warm platter with any of the traditional wines.*

# Stuffed Veal Breast II

    1 breast of veal (8 to 10 pounds)
    1 pound boneless chicken, white or dark meat, cooked
        or uncooked, coarsely chopped
    ½ cup water
    2 pounds matzos
    1 cup chicken fat, melted
    2 eggs, beaten
    1 teaspoon sage
    1 teaspoon thyme
    ½ lemon peel, grated
    4 tablespoons parsley, chopped
    1 teaspoon fresh dill weed
    1 teaspoon salt
    ½ teaspoon pepper
    2 medium-sized onions, coarsely chopped

Have the butcher prepare the breast of veal for stuffing by cracking but not removing bones and cutting the deep, large pocket in the breast to extend across the width.

Preheat the oven to 325°F. In a large bowl, moisten the matzos with the water and crumble them. Melt the chicken fat in a small pan. Pour the melted fat and chopped chicken into the bowl with the matzos. Add all the other ingredients except the onions and mix thoroughly. Stuff the mixture into the pocket of the veal breast firmly but not too tightly and close with thread or small skewers. Line the bottom of a shallow roasting pan with the chopped onions and place the stuffed breast, bone side up, on top. Roast for 1 hour, then turn over and continue cooking for another 1½ hours.

SERVES 6 TO 8.

*It is traditional in some homes to serve lamb bones with the veal, symbolizing the original Passover lamb. Bake the lamb bones in the oven for ½ hour at 325°F before serving.*

# Veal with Fig Sauce

    1 leg of veal or shoulder of boneless veal neck
       (5 to 7 pounds)
    2 pounds figs (fresh, canned, or dried)
    2 cups white wine
    8 peppercorns
      Water
    ½ cup honey

Preheat the oven to 375°F. Place the veal in a deep roasting pan, surrounding it with the figs. Put in the white wine and peppercorns and then add enough water to cover the figs. Bake for 1½ hours, checking frequently. If the liquid is evaporating, add more water and wine to keep the figs covered.

Remove the veal from the roasting pan and keep warm in a heated oven. Add the honey to the roasting pan, stir well, and return to the oven. Simmer for 15 minutes or until the sauce begins to thicken. Return the veal to the roasting pan in the oven for 10 minutes, stirring the sauce. Remove the veal to a serving platter with the figs. Pour the sauce into a gravy boat and serve on the side.

SERVES 6 TO 8.

# Baked Chicken Paprika

>2 frying or roasting chickens (2½ to 3 pounds each),
>    cut up
>2 eggs
>½ teaspoon onion salt
>2 tablespoons lemon juice
>1 teaspoon salt
>2 tablespoons paprika
>½ cup flour
>5 cups cornflakes, crumbled
>½ cup margarine

Preheat the oven to 350°F. Moisten the chicken pieces with water and then dry. Beat the eggs with the onion salt, lemon juice, salt, and paprika. Spread a pastry board with the flour and roll the chicken pieces in it. Then dip them into the egg mixture. Put the crumbled cornflakes into a large bowl and dip each floured chicken piece in them.

Melt the margarine in a roasting pan and place the chicken, skin side down, in the pan. Bake for 30 minutes. Turn over the chicken pieces and bake for 30 minutes longer or until the chicken is tender.

SERVES 4.

# Chicken Roasted in Wine Sauce

Sukkot, the Festival of the Tabernacles, commemorates the wanderings of the Children of Israel in the desert. A miniature *sukkah*, or hut, is built and is traditionally decorated with myrtle, palm shoots, lemon, willow twigs, and branches. For seven days, the family symbolically eats within the hut as did the Israelites in their wanderings.

        1 large roasting chicken (4 to 7 pounds)
        1 tablespoon salt
    ½ teaspoon pepper
        1 cup Burgundy wine
        1 teaspoon basil
        1 teaspoon thyme
        1 teaspoon garlic, crushed
        1 teaspoon marjoram
    ¼ cup honey

Preheat the oven to 400°F. Mix the salt and pepper and sprinkle the inside and outside of the chicken. Place the chicken in a deep roasting pan. In a large bowl, mix the wine with all the other ingredients, blending thoroughly. Pour over the chicken, coating it well, and let the remainder fill the bottom of the pan. Roast for 1½ to 2 hours or until the chicken is tender. Baste frequently with the liquid in the pan.

SERVES 6.

*A Carmel Sauterne goes well with this dish.*

# Honey-Baked Chicken

Yom Kippur is a sacred day of fasting, but the meal at the end is a special one, for the Talmud says it is as much a *mitzvah*, or commandment, to feast afterward as it is to fast on Yom Kippur. When the meal ends, the head of the family traditionally uses a feather to place a bit of honey in each corner of the house, voicing the wish: "May all in this house have a sweet year."

>     1 roasting chicken, cut into serving-size pieces
>     1 teaspoon salt
>     ½ teaspoon pepper
>     ½ cup flour
>     8 tablespoons margarine
>     ½ cup honey
>     2 tablespoons lemon juice
>     2 tablespoons soy sauce

Preheat the oven to 350°F. Moisten the chicken pieces with water and then drain for a few minutes. Mix the salt, pepper, and flour together and pour into a plastic or paper bag. Put the chicken pieces, a few at a time, into the bag and shake well until each piece is coated with the flour.

In a baking dish, melt 4 tablespoons of the margarine and put the chicken pieces in one at a time, turning to coat both sides with the melted margarine. Then place all the pieces, skin side down, in a single layer. Bake for 30 minutes.

In a separate pan, melt the rest of the margarine and add the honey, lemon juice, and soy sauce. Cook over a low heat, stirring until the mixture is well blended.

Turn the chicken pieces in the baking dish and pour the honey mixture over all. Return to the oven and cook for another 40 minutes, until the chicken pieces are tender and well glazed. Baste frequently with the liquid in the dish.

SERVES 4.

*Serve with a side dish of broccoli and a dry white wine.*

# 7
# AMERICA THE BOUNTIFUL

THE art of cooking in America has often been taken to task, sometimes by those who should know better. Sophisticates have deplored the lack of an American cuisine in the gourmet sense of the term. It is an unfair and largely invalid indictment which Americans themselves have aided by feeling that American cooking is merely an echo of cuisines from everywhere else, a sort of culinary patchwork quilt. This assumption is only true in part and, as we have seen, many factors go into shaping a country's cuisine.

The native riches of America were a chef's treasure house. Despite the severe winters and hostile Indians, the earliest settlers found almost every kind of game available. The land was full of rich opportunity for growing almost every kind of foodstuff. The temperate climate, the virgin forests, the fresh waterways, and the unspoiled soil were a natural storehouse. No conquerors were needed to return with new meats, new dishes, or new foods. America was no barren land, arid, harsh, and fit only for raising goats and sheep. Virtually everything was there, waiting to be hunted, trapped, planted, and nurtured.

That such a rich larder did not produce a cuisine of gourmet proportions is, of course, the basis for the indictment of American cuisine. But the early centuries of America saw a people constantly on the move, first into Virginia and Massachusetts, then into the untamed wilderness. Pioneering, not the pleasures of the palate, held the minds and energies of those early Americans. Although those who immigrated or fled to America brought with them the tastes and gastronomy of their native lands, survival and movement were their first considerations. In the pressures of such an exploding climate, culinary heritage was often all but lost. Therefore, the emergence of a truly American, native cuisine, an American approach to food, was a slow process. Moreover, there were no kings or emperors to command fancy dishes, no pharaohs and Caesars to give lavish two-day banquets requiring the skills and inventiveness of grand chefs.

Creative American cuisine and a native appreciation for

fine cooking probably began to emerge with the era of the powerful land barons and the railroad, steel, and industrial magnates. These men were the first American potentates, and they entertained with the opulent splendor requiring the services of fine chefs. That era saw the onset of a new leisure and attention to the subtleties of dining in America. An example of this is the crown roast, most often thought to be the invention of some European chef for his royal patron. But the crown roast is American in origin and seems to have made its appearance during the last half of the nineteenth century, no doubt to honor a merchant tycoon or a wealthy landholder—a crown for a commoner and entirely fitting for a country that had chosen democracy over monarchy.

But the heritage of the first Americans was not entirely lost in their new kitchens. As wave after wave of pioneering immigrants came to the new land of opportunity, they brought the culinary echoes of their homelands: of France in the dishes of the Louisiana territory; of Spain in Texas, the Southwest, and California; of England in the Northeast and along the Atlantic provinces; and of Germany and Scandinavia in Pennsylvania, the Ohio River valley, and the great Midwest. But from the New England boiled dinner to the Jambalaya of New Orleans, an indigenous and native style of cooking began to evolve blending many different backgrounds into a new homogeneity.

One element above all else came to distinguish American cuisine from all others. Meat and meat dishes were the very heart, the very central core of the American style. The meat of the land, the air, and the sea had always been basic to American cuisine. It was a robust, forthright approach to meat, one in which the meat itself was the core of the dish and not accompanying sauces or surrounding embellishments. This dominant theme of American cooking and eating was a natural result of the bounty of the land. Wild pig, deer, elk, bear, wild sheep, buffalo, squirrel, opossum, raccoon, ox, turkey, grouse, quail, partridge, goose, duck, pigeon, and pheasant were only a few of the meats available to the early Americans. Soon, herds of domesticated pigs were driven westward with almost every covered wagon, the cows being used mostly for milk production. European visitors to the new land invariably returned home in wonderment at the consumption of meat by Americans. When Anthony Trollope visited America in the mid-nineteenth century, he returned to England astounded by the fact that the Irish laborers in New York, Ohio, Michigan, and Illinois dined on meat every day of the week and that even the boarding-houses of the working class had meat at every main meal and often at breakfast.

But the myth that Americans did not appreciate gourmet dining and were a nation of limited if not Neanderthal culinary tastes still persists. All myths die hard. Modern Americans like to think that gastronomically, America has matured into a land of gourmets. True, the last twenty-five years have seen a tremendous increase in American interest in international cooking, but a quick glance backward is both illuminating and educating. The menu of the famed Mobile, Alabama hotel, the Battle House, in 1857, lists the following dishes:

MEATS—BOILED:

Ham
Tongue
Corned Beef & Cabbage
Corned Tongue
Turkey & Oysters
Calf's Head Brain Sauce

SIDE DISHES:

Sirloin of Beef, Piquant Sauce
Currie of Beef
Blanquette of Turkey Wings
Musette of Mutton, Tomato Sauce
Calf's Head, Italienne Sauce
Tripe à la Lyonnaise
Pork Cutlets Breaded
Boiled Hominey

ROASTS:

| | |
|---|---|
| Beef | Pork |
| Chicken | Leg of Mutton |
| Turkey | Veal |

Duffield's Ham—Champagne Sauce

The menu also carried a selection of 22 Madeiras, 19 sherries, 15 German wines (Hocks), 3 Burgundies, 3 ports, 5 Sauternes, 15 clarets, and 8 champagnes. All in all, that menu hardly reflected a restaurant catering to a nation of limited gourmet tastes. Perhaps even more revealing is the dining car menu of the Chicago and Northwestern Railroad of 1870:

HOT ENTRÉES:    Lamb Cutlets, à la Soubise
Sweetbreads, Braised with Mushrooms
Young Chickens, Sauté à l'Augerienne
Frogs Legs Fried in Butter

COLD ENTRÉES:    Boned Turkey
Breast of Chicken
Lambs' Tongues
Lobster Salad
Bread of Fowl's Liver, à la American

ROASTS:    English Ribs of Beef
Young Turkey, Cranberry Sauce
Stuffed Young Chicken
Loin of Veal, Macedonian Style
Saddle of Southdown Mutton with Red Currant Jelly
Louisville Ham with Champagne Sauce
Spring Lamb, Mint Sauce
Domestic Duck

GAME:    Saddle of Venison with Currant Jelly
Red Head and Canvasback Duck
Illinois Grouse with Jelly
Broiled Quail on Toast
Roast Young Prairie Chicken with Grape Jelly
Broiled Young Pigeon

The menus listed were not rarities. Those at the St. Nicholas Hotel in New York, the Tremont House in Chicago, and the great hotels of Boston and Cleveland and Detroit all showed the same magnificent range and sophistication and the same emphasis on the great meat dishes. By the nineteenth century, America had developed its own cuisine and appreciation for fine dining while raising the eminence of meat dishes to a place unrivaled even by the Englishman's love of roast beef.

It is fitting that America today is the leader in home barbecue cooking, for the roasting of meat over outdoor and indoor fires was the basic method of cooking for early American families. The first barbecue goes back to that Paleolithic chef who charred the first mastodon shank. That the most technologically advanced nation is today's chief exponent of that very same, basic cookery is conclusive proof of the unchanging love affair of man, maid, and meat, served in all its forms and prepared in all its ways.

# Steak and 30-Penny Potatoes

The cooks on the old railroad work gangs used to use this method of getting their potatoes cooked through and especially flaky to go with the meat served to the workmen.

> 1 porterhouse steak, 1½ to 2 inches thick
> 6 large baking potatoes
> 6 thirty-penny nails (these are approximately 5½ inches long and thick)
> Freshly ground pepper to taste
> Salt to taste
> 1 garlic clove, minced, or garlic powder to taste
> 1 tablespoon lemon juice

Have the butcher score the fat around the outer edges of the steak. Set the steak aside and prepare the potatoes.

Into each potato run 1 thirty-penny nail lengthwise. The head and a little of the tip of the nail should protrude from the potato. Bake the potatoes in a 400°F oven for approximately 45 minutes. The nail aids the potato in baking from the center out as well as the outside in, making a particularly flaky potato.

When the potatoes are almost done, season the steak on one side with pepper, salt, and garlic. Rub the lemon juice into the outer, scored fat and place in the broiler for 10 to 12 minutes. Turn the steak over, season the other side, and broil for another 10 to 12 minutes.

Serve the potatoes with the steak, leaving the nails in. When the potato is cut open for buttering, the nail will come out easily.

SERVES 2 TO 3.

# Stuffed Beef

In the December 1890 issue of *Housewife*, Anna Alexander Cameron offered this recipe. We give it here with its original charm and add only the suggestions to help the modern cook fill the ingredients best.

"Have ready a handsome roasting piece of beef that has hung for several days. [Use a 4-bone, standing rib roast.]

"Mix a savory stuffing as follows: Mince fine an onion about the size of a hen's egg and one pound of fat pork. Add one teaspoon of finely powdered thyme, one of savory, one of celery seed, one blade of mace, six cloves and 12 grains of allspice, all finely pounded. Mix thoroughly. [For the fat pork, have butcher grind it or do it at home in a grinder or food processor. Use thyme, savory, celery seed, and salt as directed. For the mace, use ½ teaspoon ground; for the cloves, use ½ teaspoon ground; for the allspice, use ½ teaspoon ground.]

"Lay beef in pan in which it is to be roasted and with a sharp-pointed knife make incisions all over it. Stick the knife in deep and twist it around so as to make the place large enough to hold the stuffing. Into each place sprinkle a little salt and black pepper and a very thin pinch of Cayenne pepper. Stuff the places as full as possible with the stuffing. Rub the meat over with melted butter, dredge thickly with flour.

"Put two quarts of water in the pan and set it in the oven. Allow a quarter of an hour to each pound. Ladle up the gravy over the meat constantly and dredge in flour a second time. It should be a rich brown when done but should be slightly rare, on no account overdone. This beef is delicious when cold." [For a 6-pound roast, bake for 1½ hours at 350°F; for an 8-pound roast, 2 hours. Put in enough water to cover no more than halfway up the side of the roast. Baste occasionally and again sprinkle lightly with flour halfway through the roasting time.]

SERVES 6 TO 10.

# Rotisserie Roast Beef

> 1 beef prime rib roast or sirloin roast (4 to 7 pounds),
> boneless
> 1½ cups red wine
> ¼ cup salad oil
> 1 tablespoon lemon juice
> 1 tablespoon salt
> ½ tablespoon pepper
> 1 tablespoon cornmeal

Make a marinade of the wine, salad oil, and lemon juice. Pour into a dish large enough to accommodate the beef and marinate overnight, turning several times.

Remove the meat and reserve the marinade. Season the top and all the sides of the beef (but not the ends) with the salt and pepper, then sprinkle on the cornmeal to help create a crust. Insert the beef in a rotisserie, adjusting the rods. The meat should turn only with the rotation of the rod. Roast at a low to medium heat for 15 minutes per pound for rare, 18 minutes per pound for medium, or 20 minutes per pound for well-done.

Brush frequently with the marinade while roasting. When ready to serve the roast, heat with the marinade in a saucepan and serve in a gravy boat on the side.

SERVES 10.

*A cold sparkling Burgundy is excellent with this roast.*

# Brisket of Beef

An 1890 recipe for pot roast reads, "the brisket of beef, which sells for five cents a pound, is generally used." Although prices are somewhat higher these days, brisket is still an economical piece of meat for family dinners.

        1 brisket of beef (5 to 6 pounds)
        ½ tablespoon pepper, freshly ground
        4 tablespoons salad oil
        4 medium-sized onions, chopped
        1 medium-sized green pepper
        2 stalks celery, chopped
        9 peppercorns
        12 mushrooms, thinly sliced
        3 shallots, chopped
        ½ teaspoon tarragon

Sprinkle the brisket with the freshly ground pepper. Heat the oil in a heavy casserole or kettle and put the brisket in it. Brown well on all sides and remove from the kettle. In the same oil, brown the onions, green pepper, and celery. Reduce the heat and return the meat to the kettle. Add the peppercorns and cover. Simmer gently for approximately 3 hours.

Remove the brisket and place in an oven-proof serving dish. Preheat the oven to 350°F. Skim the fat from the gravy and pour the fat into a small skillet. Pour the skimmed gravy over the brisket. Add the mushrooms, shallots, and tarragon to the skillet containing the fat, sauté until softened, and pour over the brisket. Place the dish in the oven for 20 to 30 minutes.

Serves 6 to 8.

*Mashed potatoes and a green salad go well with this. Add a robust Burgundy.*

# Soupy Beef Stew

This dish was created by Leon Lobel to introduce oxtails into the family menu alongside other meat. Today, this recipe for a large family is enjoyed just as much by his family as is prime ribs of beef.

        5 large oxtails
        5 pounds beef chuck or bottom round
        4 cups water
        4 large onions, chopped
        8 stalks celery, chopped
       10 cloves garlic, finely chopped
        1 small bunch parsley
        6 sprigs dill weed
        6 scallions
       ¼ teaspoon basil
       ¼ teaspoon caraway seed
       ¼ teaspoon thyme
       ½ teaspoon oregano
        3 large pinches chili powder
        2 large pinches red pepper (cayenne)
        1 teaspoon black pepper
        1 tablespoon salt (may be omitted if on a salt-free diet)
        1 cup barley
        2 small cans (3 oz. each) tomato paste
          Water
       ¾ pound fresh green peas, shelled
        8 carrots, quartered
       ½ pound string beans
        4 large potatoes, peeled and cut into eighths

Have the butcher remove all the fat from the oxtails and cut the joints into the size of beef stew cubes. Have the chuck or bottom round cut into 2-inch cubes.

In a 10-quart kettle, boil the 4 cups of water, then lower the heat and put in all the ingredients up to and including the salt but excluding the meat. (Add 3 more pinches of chili powder if the salt is omitted.) Mix thoroughly and then add the barley. Mix thoroughly again.

Add the 2 cans of tomato paste. Then half-fill the cans with hot water, add to the pot, and mix once again. Add the meat, stir in well, and cook over a low heat for 2½ hours, stirring occasionally. Uncover, add the rest of the ingredients, and stir thoroughly. Cover and continue cooking over a low heat for 1½ to 2 hours longer.

SERVES 12 TO 18.

*A spinach and mushroom salad, cornbread, and beer complete the dish. It can be chilled in the refrigerator for 2 to 3 days before using. It can also be frozen in foil-covered baking pans for future use, ready to pop into the oven. Remove from the freezer the night before and heat in oven for 45 minutes to 1 hour.*

# Pazole

The missionaries who came to southern California in the 1700s set up self-sufficient missions after the European fashion. The padres had their own goats, sheep, pigs, and wheat and vegetable gardens. The kitchen was called the *pazolera*, and a one-kettle meal called *pazole* was a favorite dish.

    1½ pounds beef chuck or round, cut into small cubes
    1 pound pork shoulder or loin, cut into small cubes
       Salt and pepper to taste
    ½ stick butter
    2 onions, chopped
    2 cloves garlic, coarsely chopped
    1 green or red pepper cut into short lengths after
       coring
    6 tomatoes, cut into quarters
    4 ounces tomato paste
    3 cups water
    1 pound baked beans (any variety)
    1 pound green olives, pitted and halved
    1 can (8 ounces) pimientos
    1½ pounds peas, fresh or frozen
    ¼ cup flour

In a very large kettle, place the cubed beef and pork and brown in the butter. Season with the salt and pepper while browning. When the meat cubes are browned on all sides, add the onions, garlic, and pepper and sauté gently. Add the tomatoes, tomato paste, and 2 cups of the water. Cover and simmer for 2½ hours. Add more water if needed.

Uncover and stir in the baked beans, olives, pimientos, and peas. Mix well and continue simmering, covered, for another 30 minutes. Taste and add more salt and pepper if needed. Mix the remaining 1 cup of water with the flour to form a thin paste and add it to the pot a little at a time, stirring constantly. When the paste is blended in, cover and simmer for 15 minutes longer.

SERVES 6.

*Serve over white rice and accompany with a green salad and a dry red wine.*

# Texas Casserole

> 2 pounds beef chuck or round, as lean as possible
> 5 tablespoons butter
> 1 medium-sized onion, chopped
> 1 tablespoon chili powder
> ¼ cup tomato paste
> 6 tomatoes, cut into quarters
> 1 cup green olives, pitted and halved
> 1¼ cups sharp Cheddar cheese, grated
> 1 can (15 ounces) red kidney beans
> 1 package (12 ounces) egg noodles, medium-sized
> 1 cup water

Have the beef minced (cut into very small, very fine pieces), not ground. In a skillet, brown the minced beef in 3 tablespoons of the butter and set aside. In the remaining 2 tablespoons of the butter, sauté the onion until it is soft. Add to the meat and turn the mixture into a casserole. Add the chili powder, tomato paste, tomatoes, and olives. Stir well to mix, then add the cheese and kidney beans. Mix thoroughly once again. Preheat the oven to 350°F.

Cook the noodles according to the directions on the package, drain, and mix into the casserole. Add the 1 cup of water and bake, covered, for 30 to 40 minutes or until done.

SERVES 6.

*A cold light beer goes well with this.*

# Chili con Carne

The first Spanish cookbook was printed in 1467, soon after the invention of the printing press. Called *Lubre de Coch*, it was first printed in the Catalan dialect, but soon was published in the Castilian dialect. Spanish conquistadores carried it all over the world. This recipe was brought here, and it became part of the New World's cooking.

1½ pounds beef chuck, cut into small cubes
    (approximately ¼ inch)
½ pound pork loin or shoulder, cut into small cubes
    (smaller than ½ inch)
2 tablespoons beef suet or lard
1 large onion, finely chopped
1 leek, chopped
3 cloves garlic, minced
1 can (16 ounces) tomatoes or 9 ripe fresh tomatoes
¼ cup chili powder
2½ cups water
3 bay leaves
1 tablespoon oregano
1 teaspoon cumin
1 can (16 ounces) red kidney beans

In a large pot, melt the suet and sauté the onion, leek, and garlic for 5 minutes. Add the canned tomatoes. (If you are using fresh tomatoes, cut them into quarters and press through a large sieve.) Add the chili powder and 1 cup of the water and mix well. Add the meat, bay leaves, oregano, and cumin and pour in the remaining water.

Stir everything together thoroughly. Simmer for 1½ to 2 hours, adding more water if necessary.

Heat the red kidney beans in a separate pan when casserole is ready. Stir in the heated beans, simmer for 1 minute, and then serve.

SERVES 6.

# Beef, Beans, and Biscuits

This recipe is a one-kettle dish that you can use for a barbecue.

> 2 pounds beef chuck or round, finely chopped but not
>     ground
> 9 slices bacon
> 1 can (15 ounces) tomato sauce
> 1 can (15 ounces) pinto beans
> 1 can (15 ounces) pork and beans
> 1 cup barbecue sauce
> 1 tablespoon wine vinegar
> ¼ cup brown sugar
> ¼ cup dark molasses
> 1 dozen biscuits

*Biscuits*

> 2 cups sifted flour
> 2 teaspoons double-acting baking powder
> 1¼ teaspoons salt
> 1 teaspoon sugar
> 5 tablespoons butter
> 1 cup milk

Prepare the biscuits first. Sift the flour, baking powder, salt, and sugar together. Using your hands, work in the butter in small pieces until the flour mixture is a coarse blend. Add the milk and continue to mix thoroughly until the dough is smooth.

Preheat the oven to 350°F. On a lightly floured pastry board, spread the dough to a ¾-inch-thick square. Cut out 12 pieces with a round cookie cutter. Place on a buttered cookie sheet in the oven and bake for 10 to 15 minutes or until the biscuits turn golden. If commercially prepared biscuits are used, follow the directions and then add the baked biscuits to the casserole.

To prepare the beef and beans, fry the bacon in a skillet until crisp. Drain and crumble, reserve. Pour the loose liquid fat from the skillet, then brown the chopped meat in the remaining fat. Transfer the browned meat to a large kettle and add all the other ingredients except the biscuits. Mix well and sprinkle the crumbled bacon over the top.

Place the biscuits neatly on top of everything else and place the kettle over a fire on a grill  Cook over flames for 15 to 20 minutes. Test the biscuits to make certain they are hot.

SERVES 6 TO 8.

# Comanche Cutlets

The Comanche Indians used to lay a piece of meat on a flat rock and pound it almost to a pulp with another rock. In the same way they took cooked mesquite beans and made a pulp of them and then combined the two in a tribal forerunner of our hamburgers. A modern version may be made in the manner listed here.

>    1¼ pounds beef chuck or round, ground twice
>    1 can (16 ounces) red kidney beans
>    ¼ tablespoon salt
>    ¼ teaspoon pepper
>    2 tablespoons butter

Pour the kidney beans into a mixing bowl. Using a fork or potato masher, make a pulp out of the beans. Use the liquid from the beans and mix well. (Do not use a food processor or blender, as it would make too smooth a purée.)

Season hamburger meat with the salt and pepper, add to the bowl, and mix thoroughly with the kidney bean pulp. Shape into meat patties and fry in the butter.

SERVES 3 TO 4.

*Serve on hamburger rolls with onions or any relish normally used with hamburgers.*

# Meatloaf Ring

1½ pounds beef chuck, ground
½ pound pork, ground
½ pound veal, ground
1 cup bread crumbs
1 egg
½ cup milk
½ teaspoon salt
¼ teaspoon pepper
1 small onion, minced
1 dash garlic (powder) to taste
1 tablespoon oregano
1½ tablespoons Worcestershire sauce
1 teaspoon dry mustard
Butter or shortening
¼ cup tomato paste
¼ cup water

A ring mold is needed for this dish. Mix the ground meats together in a large bowl. Then mix in the bread crumbs, egg, and milk. Mix well and add the salt, pepper, onion, garlic, oregano, Worcestershire sauce, and dry mustard. Mix everything together thoroughly.

Grease the ring mold with butter or shortening on both sides of the ring and on the bottom. Spread the meatloaf mixture evenly into the mold. In a small bowl, blend the tomato paste and water and spread over the top of the meatloaf in the mold.

Bake in a 350°F oven for 1 hour. To serve, turn the mold upside down and carefully ease out of the meatloaf ring.

SERVES 6.

*Fill the center of the ring with creamed carrots.*

# Chuckwagon Hamburger

There are hundreds and hundreds of variations on the hamburger today. The men who accompanied the great cattle drives as cooks had to cook things simply. The result was most often the best way to present meat, retaining the purity of its flavor without stuffings, embellishments, or unnecessary flavorings.

> 1½ pounds beef chuck, round, or sirloin tip
> 3 tablespoons butter (no substitutes)
> 1 teaspoon salt
> 1 teaspoon pepper
> 4 slices bread or 4 hamburger buns

Have the butcher grind the meat coarsely. In a large skillet, melt the butter until it turns brown. Mix the salt and pepper together and season the meat before making it into hamburger patties.

Make the patties and flatten them under wax paper. (Chuckwagon cooks believed strongly that thick hamburgers dry out.) Place the flat hamburgers into the browned butter. Cook gently over a low heat, turning them often until they are well done. Remove the hamburgers and place the slices of bread in the skillet. (If hamburger buns are used, place the cut side of the bun into the juices of the skillet; however, one slice of bread was the way the old chuckwagon cooks served hamburgers.) Fry the bread in the juices for 1 minute on 1 side only and remove. Place the hamburgers on the fried side.

Serves 4.

*Serve with mustard, pickle, and relish on the side.*

# Burritos

In 1769, Father Juan Crespi established a mission at a little town he named Nuestra Señora la Reina de Los Angeles. Besides teaching the people how to make cheese, Father Crespi also created a dish he called *Burritos,* after the little burros that so loved the wheat he grew.

    2 pounds beef chuck or round, ground
    ½ tablespoon salt
    ½ teaspoon cayenne pepper
    ½ cup cornmeal
    2 cups white flour
    2 teaspoons salt
      Cold water
    ¼ cup shortening, soft or melted
      Pinch of shortening or ½ tablespoon butter
    1 can (15 ounces) red kidney beans
    ½ cup Cheddar cheese, grated or finely chopped

Season the meat with salt and cayenne pepper and set aside. In a mixing bowl, mix the cornmeal, white flour, and salt. Gradually pour in enough cold water to form a smooth batter. Add the shortening and stir again to keep the batter smooth.

In a skillet, take a pinch of shortening or ½ tablespoon of butter and sauté the ground beef. When it is half-cooked, add the red kidney beans and continue to cook, stirring to separate the meat. Add the Cheddar cheese at the very last moment.

Pour the cornmeal and flour batter in a separate skillet, forming thin pancakes about 6 inches in diameter. Fry over a medium heat until done. Place a portion of the meat mixture into the center of each pancake, fold over, and serve at once.

SERVES 4 TO 5.

# Chipped Beef and Sherry Sauce

> 1 pound chipped beef
>   Boiling water
> 2 tablespoons butter
> 2 tablespoons flour
> ¼ teaspoon salt
> ⅛ teaspoon pepper
> 1 cup chicken bouillon
> ½ cup heavy cream
> ¼ cup sherry

Cover the chipped beef with boiling water and simmer for 20 minutes in the pot. Drain the water from the pot and keep the beef warm.

Melt the butter in the top of a double boiler, remove from heat, and stir in the flour, salt, and pepper. Add the chicken bouillon, return to the heat, and cook, stirring constantly, until the sauce thickens. Simmer, covered, for another 5 minutes. Then add the heavy cream and sherry and heat, stirring, for another 3 minutes. Serve the sauce over the chipped beef.

SERVES 4.

# Calf's Liver and Onions

  1½ pounds calf's liver
  ¼ cup flour
  ½ tablespoon salt
  ½ teaspoon pepper
  4 tablespoons salad oil
  2 medium-sized onions, chopped
  ½ cup beef bouillon

Have the butcher remove all the outside skin and gristle and slice the liver very thinly. Dry the slices thoroughly. Mix the flour, salt, and pepper and sprinkle over the slices on both sides. Heat the oil in a large skillet. When hot, add the liver and sauté quickly over a medium to high heat. Remove the liver to a plate and keep warm in a heated oven. Add the onions to the oil in the skillet and brown. Add the bouillon, bring to a boil, and stir until the sauce is reduced approximately 25 percent. Pour the sauce over the liver.

SERVES 4.

*Mashed potatoes, buttered Brussels sprouts, and a dry red wine make good accompaniments.*

# Simple Beef Tongue

> 1 pickled beef tongue (5 to 6 pounds)
> Boiling water
> 2 tablespoons salt
> 12 peppercorns
> 3 bay leaves
> 1 stalk celery

Place the tongue in a large kettle and cover with boiling water, enough so that the water level is 5 inches above the tongue. Add all the other ingredients, cover, and boil briskly for 2½ to 3 hours. When the small bones at the large end of the tongue come out easily, it is cooked and ready to serve.

Remove the tongue from the kettle but keep the broth simmering. Peel the skin from the tongue, return it to the kettle to heat through, and then slice and serve.

SERVES 6 TO 8.

*Boiled potatoes with lemon butter and chives go well with boiled tongue, and always serve red wine.*

# Boiled Tongue with Cherry Sauce

    1 fresh beef tongue (5 to 6 pounds)
    1 medium-sized onion, peeled
    1 stalk celery
    2 bay leaves
    4 whole cloves
    1 tablespoon parsley, chopped
      Boiling water
    1 cup Marsala wine
      Juice of 2 oranges
      Juice of 1 lemon
    ½ teaspoon cayenne pepper
    1 teaspoon Worcestershire sauce
    ½ teaspoon salt
    ¾ cup cherries, pitted

Place the tongue in a large kettle with the onion, celery, bay leaves, cloves, and parsley. Cover with boiling water, enough so that the water level is 5 inches above the tongue, and cook briskly over a medium heat for 2½ to 3 hours. When done, remove the tongue from the kettle and peel off the skin, but keep the kettle simmering. Return the tongue to the kettle to heat through.

Pour the wine into a separate saucepan and add all the other ingredients except the cherries. Bring to a boil and continue boiling, stirring occasionally, until the sauce is reduced by approximately one-third. Add the cherries and simmer for another 2 minutes. Serve hot over the tongue, with the remainder in a gravy boat.

SERVES 6 TO 8.

# All-American Veal Loaf

3 pounds veal neck or shoulder, ground
1 cup onion soup
½ cup light cream
½ pound mushrooms, finely chopped
½ teaspoon salt
½ teaspoon pepper
½ tablespoon chervil
6 slices bacon
½ green pepper, finely chopped

Simmer the onion soup in a saucepan for 10 minutes. Then add the light cream, mushrooms, salt, pepper, and chervil. Simmer, but do not boil, for an additional 10 minutes. Remove from heat and let cool. Fry the bacon in a skillet until crisp. Drain and crumble it.

Place the veal in a large mixing bowl and add the cooled soup and mushroom mixture. Mix thoroughly and refrigerate for ½ hour. Preheat the oven to 350°F. Place the veal mixture in a greased 4-inch-by-8-inch baking pan and shape to have a slight roundness on top, resembling a loaf of bread. With a knife, make crisscross lines on the veal loaf and sprinkle the crisscrosses with the crumbled bacon and chopped green pepper. Bake for 1 hour.

SERVES 4 TO 6.

# Curry of Lamb

2 pounds boneless leg of lamb, cut into 1-inch cubes
½ cup flour
1¼ tablespoons curry powder
2 tablespoons butter
1 cup beef broth
1 cup water
1 tablespoon vegetable flakes (dried)
½ cup raisins
¼ teaspoon allspice

Season the flour with the curry powder and dredge the lamb pieces. Brown the floured lamb pieces in the butter. Add the rest of the ingredients and stir well.

Cook, covered, over a low heat for approximately 1¼ hours or until the lamb is tender. Stir frequently.

SERVES 4 TO 6.

*Serve over wild rice.*

# Barbecued Lamb Chops

8 loin or rib lamb chops, 2 inches thick
  Salt and freshly ground pepper to taste
1 can (8 ounces) tomato sauce
2 tablespoons honey
1 tablespoon onion, minced
½ teaspoon dry mustard
½ teaspoon coriander, fresh or seeds
3 tablespoons Grand Marnier

Sprinkle the chops on both sides with salt and pepper. In a mixing bowl, combine all the other ingredients and mix thoroughly. Place the chops in a flat pan, cover with the mixture, and let marinate for at least 1 hour, turning once.

Remove the chops, reserving the marinade. Place the chops on a grill and brush with the marinade. Grill 20 minutes for medium-rare or 25 to 30 minutes for well-done. Turn frequently and brush on more marinade each time.

SERVES 4.

# Seared Lamb Chops on Toast

This dish is a variation on an 1890 recipe. It can be done on a barbecue or by using the broiler flame of the oven.

    4 loin or rib lamb chops, 1½ to 2 inches thick
    1 teaspoon dry mustard
    ½ tablespoon salt
    ½ tablespoon pepper
    4 slices toast

Season the chops by rubbing the dry mustard on both sides, then sprinkle with the salt and pepper. Insert a fork into the edge of the chops, into the fatty areas if possible.

If you are barbecuing them, hold the chops close to the flame, turning constantly, until both sides of the chops are seared. Then lay the chops on a grill to cook, turning at least once, for approximately 5 minutes on each side.

If you are using the broiler, hold the chops up to the flame and sear on both sides. When seared, arrange them some 6 or 7 inches from the flame. Cook 2 to 3 minutes on each side. Serve the chops atop pieces of toast with the crusts cut off.

SERVES 2.

# Special Pork Chops

>6 loin pork chops, ¾ to 1 inch thick
>1 tablespoon salad oil
>1 large onion, chopped
>1 package (8 ounces) noodles, cooked
>1 can (8 ounces) tomato sauce
>½ tablespoon chili powder
>1½ cups water
>½ tablespoon salt

In a heavy skillet with a cover or in an oven-proof pot, brown the chops in the salad oil, turning to brown on both sides. When browned, add the chopped onion, noodles, tomato sauce, chili powder, and salt. Stir, add 1 cup of the water, and mix again.

Simmer, covered, over a very low heat, for 20 minutes. Add the remaining water, stir, and continue to simmer slowly for another 15 minutes.

SERVES 3 TO 6.

# Hawaiian Ham Steak

The pig, brought to the Hawaiian Islands by Captain Cook, quickly became the main meat of the islanders, although a small, native wild pig may have existed there before then (brought by the original Polynesian settlers around A.D. 500).

> 1½ to 2 pounds ham steak from a precooked ham,
> 1 to 1½ inches thick
> 5 slices canned pineapple with juice from can
> (1 small can)
> 2 tablespoons brown sugar
> ¾ teaspoon cinnamon

Score the fat on the edge of the ham steak to prevent the meat from curling. Place the pineapple slices on top of the ham steak and pour the juice from the pineapple over everything. Place in a baking dish and bake at 325°F, uncovered, for 20 minutes. Remove and baste with the juices in the dish. Sprinkle brown sugar over the ham and pineapple slices, then sprinkle with cinnamon.

Place the pan in the broiler and broil the meat for approximately 5 minutes or until the pineapple becomes light brown.

SERVES 4.

*Baked sweet potatoes and butter accompany this dish well, along with a green salad and a rosé wine.*

# Aloha Pork

> 1 pork roast (4 to 5 pounds), center or rolled loin
> 2 large onions, sliced
> 2 tablespoons butter
> ½ cup water
> 1 can (16 ounces) pineapple, cubed or sectioned, with juice
> 1 pound mushrooms, sliced

In a roasting pan with a cover, brown the pork roast on all sides. Remove the pork and drain on paper towels. Put the onion slices into the roasting pan and brown them in the pork fat. When browned, pour all the fat from the pan, using a sieve, keeping the onion slices in the pan. Melt the butter in the pan, return the pork, and add the water. Cook, covered, for 1½ hours over a medium heat, then add the pineapple and the juice from the can. Cover and continue cooking for 15 minutes longer, then add the mushrooms. Cook for another 15 to 20 minutes.

Remove the roast pork from the pan and put on a serving platter. Pour the sauce through a sieve and serve in a gravy boat. Serve the pineapple and mushrooms around the pork.

SERVES 4 TO 6.

*Mashed potatoes and beets complement this dish. Season the beets with butter, honey, and cinnamon. Hawaiian beer would complete the meal.*

# Hanaho Frankfurters

*Hanaho* is the Hawaiian word for "pay a return visit" or "come again."

6 frankfurters, cut into thirds, or 18 small cocktail
    franks
2 cloves garlic, finely minced
1 ginger root, finely minced
1 cup Kikkoman (soy) sauce
¼ cup sugar
18 mushroom caps
1 green pepper, cut into 18 square pieces
18 cubed pieces of pineapple
18 skewers

In a mixing bowl, combine the garlic, ginger root, Kikkoman sauce, and sugar. Marinate the frankfurters for at least 1 hour. When ready to serve, place 1 mushroom cap, 1 piece of green pepper, 1 frankfurter, and a cube of pineapple on each of 18 skewers. Broil the skewered frankfurters over an open flame or chafing dish flame, letting each person do his own.

SERVES 4.

# Chicken à la King

This is a truly American dish. It was created for the owner of the Brighton Beach Hotel, Mr. E. Clarke King, in New York in 1898 by his master chef, George Greenwald.

> 1 chicken (3½ to 4 pounds)
> 10 tablespoons butter (or 1½ sticks)
> 1 green pepper, minced
> 1½ cups mushrooms, stems and pieces, sliced
> 2 tablespoons flour
> ½ tablespoon salt
> ½ teaspoon pepper
> 2 cups light cream
> 2 egg yolks
> ½ tablespoon lemon juice
> ½ teaspoon paprika
> 4 ounces pimiento, cut up
> ¼ cup sherry

Place the chicken in a large saucepan with an inch of water and cook (covered) on top of the stove for 1 hour and 40 minutes. (Alternate method: place chicken in roasting pan with an inch of water and cook, covered, for 1½ hours.) Let the chicken cool. Remove all the skin. Bone the chicken and cut into bite-sized pieces, reserving 4 cups of meat.

Melt 2 tablespoons of the butter in a pot and add the green pepper and mushroom pieces. Sauté over a medium heat for 5 minutes and add the flour, salt, and pepper. Stir well and continue to sauté until the mixture is smooth. Add the cream and continue stirring until the sauce is thickened. Soften the remaining 8 tablespoons of butter.

Pour the sauce into the top of a double boiler and add the 4 cups of cut-up chicken. (If your double boiler is too small to accommodate the chicken along with the other ingredients, use a pot immersed halfway in a large pan of boiling water.) Keep hot in the double boiler. Beat in the softened butter and the 2 egg yolks and add the lemon juice and paprika, stirring constantly. Add the pimientos, stir, remove from the double boiler, and add the sherry. Continue to stir until smooth.

SERVES 4 TO 6.

*Serve over slices of toast.*

# Barbecued Chicken

```
    2 frying or roasting chickens (3 to 4 pounds each),
        quartered
      Olive oil
      Freshly ground black pepper
    1 cup butter
 1½ tablespoons lemon juice
   ¼ teaspoon Tabasco sauce
   ¼ teaspoon cayenne pepper, ground
   ½ cup water
    1 tablespoon flour
```

In a large, flat pan, marinate the chicken pieces in enough olive oil to cover and season liberally with the freshly ground pepper. Marinate for 2 to 3 hours.

Make the sauce before barbecuing the chicken. Melt the butter in a pan and add the lemon juice, Tabasco sauce, and cayenne pepper. Mix well. In a separate dish, mix the water and flour, then add to the butter mixture and blend until smooth. The sauce should be thin. Add more water if it thickens.

Place the chicken pieces skin side up on the grill. Cook the chicken for 10 minutes, then turn and baste with the sauce. Baste and turn every 10 minutes or so until the chicken pieces are tender, approximately 45 minutes.

SERVES 6 TO 8.

# Church Builder Chicken

The community social was the traditional way to raise money to build a church in early America, a custom that is still very much alive in many parts of the country. A recipe out of Virginia became a runaway favorite throughout much of the South and West. It came to be known as Church Builder Chicken.

        2 chickens (3 pounds each)
    1½ pounds bacon, in 1 piece
        4 pounds potatoes
        2 large onions, diced
        3 cans (15 ounces each) wax or yellow snap beans,
            undrained
        2 cans (15 ounces each) whole-kernel corn, undrained
        2 cans (15 ounces each) tomatoes, undrained
    ½ teaspoon red pepper (cayenne)
    ½ teaspoon black pepper
        2 teaspoons salt

Roast or boil the chickens until the meat can easily be removed. Remove every bit of edible meat on the chickens and cut into bite-size pieces, discarding the skin. Set the chicken aside.

Cut the bacon into ½-inch cubes and bake in the oven at 325°F until well-done. Take out and set aside. Peel the potatoes, boil them, and then mash. Sauté the diced onions in oil until soft, then mix with the mashed potatoes.

In a very large casserole or kettle, put in the canned beans, corn, and tomatoes. Sprinkle with the red and black pepper and salt and mix. Add the mashed potatoes, chicken pieces, and bacon. Mix everything well and simmer, covered, very gently for 30 minutes. The mixture should be hot and thick when served.

SERVES 8.

*Serve with biscuits or cornbread.*

# Hawaiian Curried Chicken

>1 broiler or frying chicken (3 to 4 pounds)
>5 tablespoons butter
>1 onion, chopped
>1 clove garlic, chopped
>1 teaspoon grated or dried ginger root
>1 tablespoon curry powder
>½ tablespoon brown sugar
>¼ cup flour
>2 cups chicken bouillon (or stock from cooking the chicken)

Either roast or boil the chicken. When cooked, let it cool and then remove all the meat, cutting into bite-sized pieces. Set aside.

Melt 3 tablespoons of the butter in a pot and sauté the onion, garlic, and ginger root for approximately 5 to 7 minutes over a medium heat, stirring frequently. Add the remaining butter, let it melt, and then stir in the curry powder and brown sugar. Add the flour a little at a time over a medium heat. When smooth, add the chicken bouillon or stock. Stir until smooth and beginning to thicken. Add the chicken meat and simmer for 10 to 15 minutes.

SERVES 4 TO 5.

*Serve over slices of toast. A simple spinach and mushroom salad and a white wine go well with this.*

# Chicken with Hawaiian Stuffing

> 1 large roasting chicken (4 to 6 pounds) (a 7-pound
>     capon may be substituted)
> ½ tablespoon salt
> ½ tablespoon pepper
> 6 tablespoons butter
> 1 cup white rice, uncooked
> 1 medium-sized onion, finely chopped
> 2 chicken bouillon cubes, crushed
> 3 cups water
> ¾ cup macadamia nuts, finely chopped
> ¾ cup coconut, flaked or grated

Sprinkle the chicken inside and out with the salt and pepper and set aside.

In a large pot, melt the butter and sauté the rice, stirring frequently, until the rice turns golden. Add the onion and crushed bouillon cubes and pour in the water. Stir and heat to boiling. Simmer, covered, until the rice is tender and the liquid is absorbed, approximately 20 minutes. Preheat the oven to 350°F. Mix in the macadamia nuts and coconut and stuff the chicken.

When the chicken is stuffed, roast it, breast side up, for approximately 20 minutes per pound. Raise the temperature to 400°F and roast for 20 minutes longer. Baste frequently.

SERVES 4 TO 6.

*Carrots, buttered and tossed with chives, buttered peas, and a cold white wine complete this meal.*

# Chicken Livers with Wine

In the Old West, a coward was labeled "white-livered" or "lily-livered." This was probably a carry-over from medieval times when a coward's liver was thought to contain no blood and was, therefore, white. But the pioneers made food of every part of the animals they used for survival, and dishes we now consider gourmet were commonplace then.

    1 pound chicken livers, plump and firm
    2 tablespoons butter
    ¼ tablespoon salt
    ¼ tablespoon pepper
    ½ teaspoon sage
    ¾ cup white wine
    6 shallots, chopped

Have the butcher prepare the chicken livers for cooking. Dry the livers thoroughly. Melt the butter in a skillet and brown the livers on 1 side for 4 to 5 minutes, then turn and brown the other side for the same length of time. Sprinkle with the salt, pepper, and sage. Stir, turn the livers again, and add the wine and chopped shallots. Turn down the heat and let simmer for 10 minutes, stirring occasionally.

SERVES 2.

*The livers may be served over rice or slices of white bread sautéed for a minute in the skillet juices.*

# Chicken Livers with Apple Cider

In pioneer farm homes, apple cider was far more plentiful than wine.

Using the preceding recipe, substitute ¾ cup of apple cider for the wine. Also, eliminate the shallots, replacing with one diced apple. This dish has a very different taste.

SERVES 2.

# Boiled Capon

A fondness for capon was brought to America by settlers from England.

    1 capon (6 to 8 pounds)
      Warm water
    4 carrots, peeled and cut into quarters
    1 large onion, sliced
    ½ tablespoon salt
    ½ tablespoon parsley, chopped
    ¼ teaspoon sage
    ¼ teaspoon thyme
    ¼ teaspoon allspice
    2 pounds dried prunes, pitted and cooked
    3 tablespoons butter

*Sauce*

    4 tablespoons butter
    4 tablespoons flour
    2 cups broth from cooking the capon
    ½ teaspoon pepper
    ½ tablespoon nutmeg
    1 cup heavy cream

Have the butcher prepare the capon for cooking. In a large pot with a cover, place the capon in the center. Pour enough warm water over the capon to cover. Simmer the capon for 5 minutes, then skim off any surface fat. Add the carrots, onion, and enough water to replace what has been skimmed off. Simmer for another 5 minutes and skim the surface fat once again. Then add the salt, parsley, sage, thyme, and allspice. Replace with enough water to cover the capon and cover tightly. Boil over a gentle heat, no more than simmering, for 2½ hours or until tender. Turn the capon twice during this period.

In a separate pan, melt the butter and cook the prunes. These may be set aside and held for reheating when ready to serve.

To prepare the Sauce, melt but do not brown the butter. Stir in the flour a little at a time, stirring constantly. Add the broth and continue stirring until the sauce is thickened and smooth. Add the pepper, nutmeg, and heavy cream. Stir again thoroughly and keep warm but do not allow the sauce to boil. (This can be done by placing the pan in a large pot of boiling water halfway up the sides.)

Remove the capon from the water and carefully take off as much of the skin as possible with a small knife. Reheat the prunes. Serve the capon on a platter surrounded by the carrots and the prunes. Serve the sauce separately.

SERVES 4 TO 6.

*A chilled Sauterne accompanies this dish well.*

# Roast Turkey

>     1 turkey (12 to 16 pounds)
>     ½ tablespoon salt
>     ½ teaspoon pepper
>     1 tablespoon paprika
>     1½ cups water
>     2½ cups apricot juice
>         Stuffing (according to your preference)

Pat the turkey dry, then sprinkle inside with the salt and pepper mixed together. Choose a stuffing of your preference and stuff the bird. Most people tie the cavity and legs with thread or skewers. Doing this is not necessary, and if the turkey is left untied, the stuffing may be packed in a little more fully. Preheat the oven to 400°F.

Coat the breast of the turkey with the paprika and place the bird in a large roasting pan. Add the water and apricot juice and cover. A good, covered roasting pan will make for a fine, moist bird. If no cover is available, make one of aluminum foil, but a cover is preferable for ease in removing for basting.

Roast, covered, for 4 to 5 hours, basting frequently with pan juices. The paprika coating makes it unnecessary to remove the cover for final browning. Keep covered and moist until ready to serve.

SERVES 8 TO 12.

*Some people prefer a red wine with roast turkey.*

# Turkey Pan Loaf

    3 cups cooked turkey
    ½ cup butter, melted
    1½ cups bread crumbs
    2 eggs, lightly beaten
    1 cup turkey broth (chicken bouillon may be
        substituted)
    ½ onion, minced
    1 tablespoon green pepper, minced
    ½ teaspoon sage

*Sauce (optional)*

    1 can (10 ounces) condensed Cheddar cheese soup
    1½ cups milk

Remove all the skin from the turkey and cut or grind into very fine pieces, reserving 3 cups. Put the melted butter in a large mixing bowl and add the bread crumbs. (Homemade bread crumbs, not too fine, are best.) Add the eggs and broth, mix well, and then add all the other ingredients. Mix thoroughly.

Preheat the oven to 350°F. Pour the mixture into a greased meatloaf pan at least 9 x 5 x 3 inches. Bake for 45 minutes.

A quick sauce may be made by mixing the soup with the milk in a pan over a medium heat. Stir constantly, bring to a boil, and then reduce the heat. Simmer for another few minutes, until the sauce is smooth. Pour into a gravy boat and serve with the turkey pan loaf.

SERVES 4 TO 6.

# Snowshoe Hare

The snowshoe hare is a particularly tasty meat, but this recipe can, of course, be used with any kind of rabbit.

1 snowshoe hare (or plump rabbit), cut into serving-size pieces
½ stick butter
½ teaspoon cinnamon
½ teaspoon nutmeg
1 tablespoon horseradish
1 bay leaf
¾ cup water
2 tablespoons flour

Preheat the oven to 350°F. Melt the butter in a large skillet or Dutch oven. Brown all pieces of the hare on all sides. Remove the pieces and set aside, keeping warm. Add the cinnamon, nutmeg, horseradish, and bay leaf to the pan, stir well, and set aside. Return the hare to the pan and pour the butter mixture over it. Add ½ cup of the water and bake for 1 hour.

When the hare is done, mix the flour into the remaining water, mixing thoroughly until smooth. Remove the hare to a heated serving dish and keep warm. Pour the flour mixture into the pan with the juices to make the gravy. Stir and thicken. Serve the gravy separately.

SERVES 2 TO 4.

*Mashed potatoes make a good accompanying dish; also serve a rosé wine.*

# Jack Pine Venison

The old trappers and mountain men came out of the hills only at trading time. They stayed only long enough to do their trading and then hurried back to the wilderness. A solitary, wild breed of men, they were called Jack Pine Savages, but they learned to cook well for their own survival. This recipe is a heritage left by the Jack Pine Savages.

        4 to 6 pounds shoulder or rump venison
            3 cups wine vinegar
            6 cups water
            1 tablespoon salt
            6 bay leaves
           10 whole cloves
            ½ pound bacon, sliced
            6 thin strips beef suet, cut into strips
            3 carrots, cut into quarters
            3 stalks celery, cut into small pieces
            2 onions, coarsely chopped
            2 rutabagas, cut into small pieces
            1 teaspoon salt
            ½ teaspoon pepper

In a large bowl, combine the wine vinegar, 3 cups of the water, salt, bay leaves, and cloves to make a marinade. With a sharp knife, make small holes an inch apart over the entire piece of venison. Place the venison in the marinade for 24 hours. (If marinade does not cover the venison, add more vinegar and water in equal parts and additional salt, until the venison is covered.)

When ready to cook, lay the beef suet and bacon over the top of the venison, covering the entire top of the meat. Preheat the oven to 325°F. In a large kettle, mix all the other ingredients, including the 3 cups of water remaining. Push aside the vegetables and set the venison in the center of the pot. Cook, covered, for at least 2½ hours. Add more water if

240 THE LOBEL BROTHERS' MEAT COOKBOOK

necessary. Serve with vegetables from the pot mixed together.

SERVES 8.

*Serve with baked or mashed potatoes and a sauce boat of red currant jelly.*

# Rotisserie Barbecue
*(Duck or Goose)*

The rotisserie is the modern American version of the old barbecue spit, and this recipe is especially designed for this twentieth century method of indoor barbecuing.

        1 duck or goose, cleaned and ready for roasting
        1 can (12 ounces) apricot nectar
        1 tablespoon apricot brandy
    ½ cup port or Marsala wine
        1 tablespoon lemon juice
        2 tablespoons salad oil
    1½ tablespoons mint flakes (optional)
        1 teaspoon salt

With a fork, prick the skin of the duck or goose all over. Make a marinade of the apricot nectar, apricot brandy, port or Marsala wine, lemon juice, oil, mint flakes, and salt. Pour into a dish large enough to hold the duck and goose. Marinate the bird overnight under an aluminum foil cover, turning once or twice.

Remove the bird, reserving the marinade. Insert the bird in a rotisserie on rods approximately 12 inches from the flame to prevent searing. The bird should turn only with the rotation of the rod. Roast at 375°F: the duck for 1½ to 2 hours; the goose for 2½ to 3 hours. Brush frequently with the marinade.

Heat the remainder of the marinade in a saucepan, stirring occasionally, and serve in a gravy boat with the bird.

SERVES 4 TO 5.

*A cold white wine should accompany your bird.*

# Sautéed Quail

Quail is finding new popularity, but it was a favorite with the early American settlers. Quail breed prolifically and grow wing quills so quickly they can fly within a week of birth.

        4 quail
        1 stick butter
        1 medium-sized onion, chopped
        ½ cup Teriyaki sauce
        ½ tablespoon garlic salt
        ¼ tablespoon salt

Have the butcher split the quails down the back. In a deep pan with a cover, sauté the quail in the butter for 5 to 7 minutes over a medium heat, turning at least once. (Sauté with the lid on.)

Add the onion and brown for an additional 3 to 5 minutes, covered. Uncover during the last minute and add the Teriyaki sauce, garlic salt, and salt. Stir, remove the quail to a serving platter, and pour the sauce over each.

SERVES 4.

*Serve with buttered string beans and a delicate white wine.*

# Quail with White Raisins

      4 quail, cleaned and prepared for cooking
      ½ tablespoon salt
      ½ teaspoon white pepper
      3 tablespoons flour
      ½ cup butter
      ¾ cup dry white wine
      1½ tablespoons lemon juice
      1 cup white raisins

Mix the salt and white pepper into the flour and rub the quail with the mixture on all sides. In a heavy casserole, melt the butter and sauté the quail on all sides, browning well until they are a deep gold in color. Add the wine and lemon juice, stir, cover, and simmer for 20 minutes.

Add the white raisins and continue simmering for another 10 minutes.

SERVES 4.

*Serve with Brussels sprouts flavored with lemon and butter, accompanied by white wine.*

# Grilled Quail

> 4 quail, split but with the halves held together
> 1½ tablespoons salt
> ½ tablespoon freshly ground pepper
> 1 stick butter
> 1 large onion, minced
> 2 tablespoons butter
> 1 cup salad croutons

Rub both sides of the split quail with the salt and pepper mixed together. Soften the butter but do not melt it. Brush ½ tablespoon of the softened butter on one side of the quail.

Place the quail, buttered side up, on a grill or under the broiler and grill for 6 minutes. Turn and brush the other side with ½ tablespoon of the butter and grill for another 6 minutes. In a separate skillet, sauté the onions in the remaining butter. Add the croutons, stir, and heat. Then make a bed of the onion-crouton mixture for each quail and place the quail on top.

SERVES 4.

*A chilled Chablis adds zest to the quail.*

# Boneless Stuffed Quail

    4 quail
    2 cups wild rice
    ½ cup butter
    1 tablespoon sage
    ¾ teaspoon salt
    ½ teaspoon black pepper

Have the butcher bone the quail. Cook the wild rice according to the directions on the package and keep warm over a low heat. Melt the butter in a separate pan, add the sage and ¼ teaspoon of salt, and mix thoroughly. Drain the rice, pour the sage butter over it, and mix thoroughly.

Preheat the oven to 350°F. Stuff the boned quail with the wild rice mixture, not too tightly. Rub the outside of the birds with the pepper and ½ tablespoon of salt mixed together. Place the quail in a roasting pan and bake for 20 minutes or until tender.

SERVES 2.

*Serve with potatoes quartered, boiled, and seasoned with butter, chives, and lemon juice. A cold dry white wine should accompany this dish.*

# Piquant Squab

The hardy squab, or pigeon, makes a very tasty dish.

6 squab, cleaned and split into halves
2 cups salad oil
½ tablespoon salt
½ teaspoon pepper
¼ cup onion, chopped
¼ teaspoon basil
½ cup chicken bouillon
2 cans, small, or ½ pound fresh mushrooms, cooked
½ cup white wine

Make a marinade of the oil, salt, pepper, onion, and basil in a roomy flat dish or pan. Place the squab halves in the marinade for 3 hours, turning occasionally and stirring the marinade at the same time. Drain the squab halves and pour the marinade into a large kettle or oven-proof casserole.

Heat over a medium heat until the marinade simmers, then place the squab sections in the pot and cook, covered, over a medium heat for 15 minutes, stirring occasionally. Mix the mushrooms, chicken bouillon, and white wine in a bowl and pour over the squab pieces. Cook gently for another 45 minutes, basting frequently.

SERVES 6.

*Serve squab sections over white rice bed. A rosé can be served with this dish.*

# Pheasant with Apples

      1 pheasant, cleaned and ready to roast
      4 tablespoons butter
      2 tablespoons salad oil
      ½ piece or package bacon (½ pound), diced
      2 small onions, minced
      4 cloves garlic
      4 apples, peeled, cored, and thickly sliced
      ⅓ cup Grand Marnier
   1½ cups light cream
      ½ teaspoon salt
      ¼ teaspoon pepper

Melt the butter and oil together in a flame-proof casserole. Sauté the diced bacon, onions, and garlic until softened and golden. Remove the bacon, garlic, and onions, using a slotted spoon, and reserve.

Put the pheasant in the casserole and brown on all sides.

Remove and keep warm in a 175°F oven. Place the apple slices in a casserole and sauté until they turn golden. Move the apple slices to the sides to make room for the pheasant. Return the pheasant to the casserole in the center of the apple slices, add the bacon, garlic, and onion, and pour in the Grand Marnier. Pour the Grand Marnier over the vegetables, not the pheasant. Simmer, covered, for 10 minutes. Add the light cream, stirring in around the casserole, sprinkle with the salt and pepper. Cover and cook in a 275°F oven until tender, approximately 1 hour.

SERVES 2.

*A cold Sauterne goes well with pheasant.*

# INDEX